Patience, my foot!

Learning God's Patience
Through Life's Difficulties

Patience, my foot!

Michael LeFan

COLLEGE PRESS
PUBLISHING COMPANY
Joplin, Missouri

Unless otherwise noted all
Scripture taken from the HOLY BIBLE,
NEW INTERNATIONAL VERSION®.
Copyright © 1973, 1978, 1984 by
International Bible Society. Used by
permission of Zondervan Publishing House.
All rights reserved.

Words of song TEACH ME, LORD, TO WAIT by Stuart Hamblen
© 1953, renewed 1981 by Hamblen Music Co., P.O. Box
1937, Canyon Country, CA 91386. Sheet music available.

Printed and Bound in the United States of America.

Library of Congress Catalog Card Number 93-73257
International Standard Book Number: 0-89900-619-1

Dedication

There are people in this world who make it terrifically tough for others to be patient (you folks know who you are). If you've ever been chided that "You would try the patience of Job" then you may be one of those burrs who gets under people's saddle blankets. On the other hand, there are people in the world whose Christ-like spirits make it exceptionally easy for others to have no need of unusual degrees of patience. This book is dedicated to each of you who is patient (thus not requiring others to exercise their forbearance), and it is dedicated to the great crowd of the rest of us who want to be that way.

Table of Contents

Foreword

Many of us heard from our mothers: "Cleanliness is next to godliness"! But according to 2 Peter it is patience which comes just before godliness. Wherever we may rank patience in relation to divinity, it is clearly one of the most missing virtues in our own time. Instead, we are flooded with books teaching us how to be more efficient rather than more patient (*The One-Minute Manager* comes to mind). Patience is one of the most unsought goals in the nation of "Fast Food" (which, someone once quipped, is neither).

The author of this creative book on patience, Michael LeFan, is one of the most impressive people that I have known, and is perhaps the most qualified person I know to write on the topic of patience. This book is witty, insightful, and instructive. But most of all, it is readable while being all of these.

Because of Michael's illness, which restricts his physical mobility, one's first impression at meeting him is necessarily focused on those limitations. I did that too, when we first met almost 20 years ago. But to focus upon Mike's very real physical limitations is to miss what is most important about him. It is neither those limitations, nor his ingenuity and success in dealing with them, which I find most impressive. It is Mike's dedication to God and his breadth of knowledge which is most outstanding.

All of us right-handers who have ever tried to use a screwdriver with our left hand (and, I assume, vice versa) appreciate the patience required to successfully master some skill that is "unnatural" for us. Mike LeFan has developed a dexterity and has made accomplishments with his left foot that any who have not witnessed it will find incredible (in the literal sense—not possible to believe!).

Mike tells something of his personal story in the opening chapter of the book. But beyond the amazing facts of his life, more impressive is his attitude in his situation. He is more cheerful, more funny, indeed, more carefree than almost anyone else I know. He is truly a person who has taken a physical challenge and made more than the most of it.

In this book on patience we will all see some of the foibles that derive from our lack of patience. To get a clearer view on the importance of patience will help us in many other areas of our life. We will understand the value of people in a better way, we will see the relative unimportance of many things which we may think are demanding, and we will value God more. You will be, I am sure, inspired by this book.

Wendell Willis, Minister
South National Church of Christ
Springfield, Missouri

CHAPTER 1

Patience–It's Only a Matter of Time

As a kid, I loved Popeye cartoons. Remember Wimpy? He was a pro at mooching hamburgers. Because he never had the money for buying a burger, Wimpy was a devotee of the soft touch. With an air of feigned haughtiness he'd promise, "I'll gladly repay you Tuesday for a hamburger today." It wasn't that Wimpy was cheap. I've thought about this, and Wimpy's real problem was impatience. He was not willing to forego immediate gratification of his hamburger craving in favor of sustained work to earn money for hamburgers at a later time. Wimpy wanted what he wanted–right now.

In the long hot August of 1954, polio was still a summertime dread all across the U.S. The Salk vaccine wouldn't be available until 1955. Since nobody was certain about how polio was transmitted from person to person, folks lived in a sort of general fear–especially through the summers, which seemed to be the disease's favorite season. Parents kept children at home, while swimming pools, movie theaters, and other public places closed, and drinking fountains were dismantled in order to curb the spread of polio. Special polio treatment centers around the nation were full of children and adults who had been infected by this virus. Many patients required iron lung machines to do their breathing for them, since polio had destroyed the nerves which control normal respiration. And in many cases, a new patient had to be placed on an iron lung waiting list—until some other patient died and no longer needed the machine.

I was eight years old and getting ready for the third grade in August of 1954 when my mother and father learned that what the doctor first diagnosed as "tonsillitis" was actually severe paralytic polio with full respiratory involvement, meningitis, and possibly encephalitis. There was no guarantee that I would live, and if I did it was certain that I'd be almost totally paralyzed. I would be able to breathe only with the aid of one of those iron lungs. Nothing could stop the inroads of the disease which was attacking me. Undoubtedly that was the worst case of "tonsillitis" in medical history. Everyone felt deep compassion for my folks, my four-year-old sister, my two month old brother, and for me, as our family faced this heartbreaking crisis. My dad was minister at what was then the Avenue G Church of Christ in Temple, Texas. The congregation rallied with support, allowing him time away to be with me in the Southwest Poliomyelitis Institute in Houston. Church members helped care for my brother and sister while my parents were frequently away over the following six months of my first hospitalization.

In the intervening years, I've talked about this period and the years of subsequent rehabilitation. As my dad, James, once said, "It seemed as though we had three choices. We could curse God for letting this happen to us and look for ways to vent our rage. We could grit our teeth and bear it. Or we could accept what life had brought our way."

The first choice is fruitless and self-destructive. The second is unproductive and debilitating. The third is the only reasonable way.

I don't say that in order to impress you. I've done nothing impressive. Rather, like the unprofitable servant of the

Scriptures, I've done only what was required of me. I relate the fact only to let you know that I have "credentials" when it comes to speaking about patience.

Again and again, life forces each of us into situations in which we have these same choices: rage and rebellion, brute endurance, or patient acceptance—the willingness that it be so. The first two, as my father knew and as I've learned, tear us apart and eventually destroy us. The only hope—my only hope—was in patient and creative acceptance. When a building is damaged by floods or storms, the disaster must be accepted before rebuilding can begin. Life's disasters must be dealt with the same way.

We must learn to face life's jolting experiences, accepting them patiently as a challenge—and not in supine resignation. Only when we yield to what we're powerless to change—only when we are willing that it be so—can we free ourselves from destructive anger, resentment, and (yes) impatience. It's no use pretending that the painful experience doesn't have us in its grasp. Ignoring it won't make it go away. If we are to live with any sense of purpose and well-being, then there must come a time when we willingly give ourselves to the situation as it is and see what we can do about remodeling it into an inhabitable condition. It's useless to curse our fate. To merely endure it is to live in drudgery. To accept life and to reach for it is the only sensible course.

This does not mean that we are to fold up like an umbrella, lay our hands in our laps, and stare piously toward heaven while we live as a Mr. Martyr or Poor Pitiful Pearl. Patient acceptance is nothing like that.

Acceptance is Michelangelo as he walked through the marble quarry, confident that if he could find the right block of marble he could fashion the masterpiece that was in his mind. Other artists had been there before him. They had selected the beautiful, majestic blocks of stone. Michelangelo found only a single, irregular marble monolith. He gazed at the piece, then he accepted it, ordering that this discarded stone be delivered to his shop. For months he chipped and chiseled at this stone, and from that jagged, misshapen hulk he created his masterwork *David*. "Its outlines," he said later, "were dictated by the imperfections of the block I worked with—the bend of the head, the twist of the body, the arm holding the sling. They were all there in the jagged, irregular piece of rock."

Not only must we seek to patiently accept the "jagged, irregular piece of rock" which life hands us, we must also develop the ability to celebrate that bequest with thanksgiving. "To be what we are, and to become what we are capable of becoming is the only end of life," said Robert Louis Stevenson. A major cause of failure and unhappiness is our unwillingness to become ourselves—to be who we are—without envy, anger, or resentment.

My polio left me totally paralyzed—almost. I needed someone else's help to eat, bathe, dress, and take care of all personal necessities. And I still need that. But as months and years passed, I found that my left leg and foot had movement, even dexterity. It began as a way to entertain myself, but over time I learned to pick up a pencil in my toes and eventually even to scribble with it. The rehabilitation professionals ignored this small capability and focused instead on teaching me to use my arms with the aid of special overhead slings. All of this required that I sit up straight, which was demanding because of my deficient breathing ability (then aided by a chest respirator device called a "shell") and because my back was weak and soon fatigued. I was more comfortable in a reclining position about halfway between sitting up and lying down. This was also the angle at which I could most effectively use my toes. So this tug-of-war went on, my occupational and physical therapists determined that I'd sit up and learn to feed myself with special utensils strapped to my useless hands, and with me equally determined to do things my way using my left foot.

How the decision was made, I don't know. Nobody that I recall ever said to me "Accept it." But at some point it must have dawned on me that my two rehab options each carried advantages and drawbacks. To sit up and use the arm slings was more "natural," but my abilities would be severely limited. On the other hand, concentrating on the dexterity of my toes offered a fuller range of possibilities even though it was not so "normal."

At some point I accepted myself as I was, for what I was, even if that didn't fit the therapists' vision of a rehabilitated person. But that was their problem. From that time on, I began developing whatever skills I could get my left foot to perform. I write with the toes of my left foot—I earned a degree in English at the University of Mary Hardin-Baylor in Belton, Texas. And I took all class notes, tests, and did other work using my toes. The choice to concentrate on using my foot has been a happy one. Ability came only when I accepted my disability.

No matter who we are or what we want to accomplish, we must begin with patient self-acceptance. If we are to fulfill our potential, first we must recognize our limitations. We have to throw off our masks, quit playing roles, and use what we have with genuineness and without excuses. Our lack of perfection doesn't matter. As Jimmy Durante said, "All of us have schnozzles. That is, we are ridiculous in one way or another: if not in our faces, then in our characters, in our minds, or in our habits. When we admit our schnozzles instead of defending them, we begin to laugh and the world laughs with us."

When we accept ourselves with patience, without feeling envy or anger toward others (including God), we are set free to begin the joyful business of living.

The Bible frequently refers to the unique roles served by various parts of our bodies. The lowly spleen can't accomplish the marvels of which the hand is capable, but it has no need to envy the hand and its skills. The eye cannot hear like an ear can, but each has its useful function in the body's over-all design. Each complements the other. Neither should diversity in the human experience cause us to feel envy, anger, or impatience. Never mind if someone else is more clever, superior, more esteemed, or more useful. What's that to us? Our job is to develop from within the best we have to offer.

We must accept today patiently. Life is now. Life is today—not in the past or the future. In the words of the song, "Yesterday's gone and tomorrow is out of sight." You want to hear a real cliche? Here it is: What is past is past. Wow! If that's where your regrets, anger, resentments, envies, and pains reside, then let them stay there. Let the past bury its dead. If you have joys, achievements, and happy experiences there, be thankful for them and think about them only so far as they give you joy today. Avoid tinting today blue with reveries of better circumstances and warm relationships which can never be again. Use the sweetness of those events to bless today—not to embitter it.

And don't lose patience with today in a fever to grasp an achievement you envision for some future time. Too many of us are marking time today in anticipation of a "better day" on some imagined tomorrow. The high schooler will be happy when he or she gets away from the prison wardens posing as parents; the college student will be happy when she has a job and family; the young married person will be happy when he has acquired some of this world's goods; the middle aged person will arrive at happiness when the bills are paid and the kids are grown; and the retiree will be happy when those thoughtless kids let him see the grandchildren more often. And on it goes. It's a mistake to think that life will really begin when . . . .

As Miguel de Cervantes, the author of *Don Quixote*, noted, on the street called "By and By" we arrive at the house named "never."

When we are impatient with today and refuse to accept it as is, we find ourselves in the situation of a persnickety old lady I read about who was boarding a train with her husband. She couldn't seem to get settled. First she put her packages on the seat beside her, then she moved them to the floor, and finally she placed them on the overhead rack. She switched the light on, then off, and then on again. She fiddled with the window shade, and had trouble getting her seat angle properly adjusted. When her husband scolded her, she said, "I want to get set so I can look at the scenery in comfort." Shaking his head, he replied, "We ain't going far, and the scenery will be long gone before you get settled down to look at it."

That's the way life is too. If you don't enjoy it as it comes to you, you'll never find enjoyment at the end of the trip either.

Life is here now, right outside the window. Learn to accept it today, in patience, because it won't come again. It's not like television, where if you miss a program you can catch it later in the reruns. Life offers no reruns. It's foolish to live your life in either a nostalgic "One Day" of the past or an impatient "Some Day" in the future. Wisdom realizes that "Today is the day that the Lord hath made." "Now" is ours to experience. Today is all that we actually possess.

Don't misunderstand. This doesn't mean that we are supposed to abandon responsibility and live in cynical hedonism—eating, drinking, and making merry, for tomorrow we die. No, the attitude we need is one that invites us to live patiently and thankfully in each day. You've heard the old saying that "Yesterday is a canceled check; tomorrow is a promissory note; today is ready cash; spend it wisely."

Dietrich Bonhoeffer, the Protestant theologian who was murdered at the hands of Hitler's Nazis, wrote in his *Letters and Papers from Prison,*

It is the mark of a grown-up man, as compared with a callow youth, that he finds his center of gravity wherever he happens to be at the moment, and however much he longs for the object of his desires, it cannot prevent him from staying at his post and doing his duty . . . . There is a wholeness about the fully grown man which makes him concentrate on the present moment.

That's what the apostle Paul meant when he wrote,

I am not saying this because I am in need, for I have learned to be content whatever the circumstances. I know what it is to be in need, and I know what it is to have plenty. I have learned the secret of being content in any and every situation, whether well fed or hungry, whether living in plenty or in want (Philippians 4:11, 12).

The measure of a mature, content (patient) person is to accept the fiery chapters of life without bitterness or complaint, to make the laughter redeem the tears, and having done it all, to triumph.

Are you a patient person? Most of us would answer, "I think so—I try to be." But sometimes we carry one image in our mind while the reality is something else.

Our congregation decided once that we would produce our own pictorial membership directory (big mistake). One of the men had a fine new Polaroid camera, which he set up in one of the church offices. The agreement was that he'd take your picture until he got a photo which satisfied you— none of those driver's license mugshots, thank you. All went reasonably well until this one lady's turn came to be in front of the camera.

The first picture was too dark, even the photographer could see that. So they made a second picture. This time she felt her hair wasn't right. Okay, so they set up for a third one (after she'd made adjustments to her coiffure, of course). Well, this one had rather harsh, unflattering shadows on her face.

By the time they'd endured eight snaps of the shutter—thanks to exaggerated wrinkles, off-center poses, and other objections—nerves were fraying a bit. "I don't know why you can't get a good picture," protested the lady.

"Ma'am," snapped the photographer, "this camera can't take what's not there."

Do you remember the first time you heard your own voice on a tape recorder? Your immediate reaction was likely to say, "That's not ME. It doesn't sound like me." And it didn't sound like you to you, because the way we hear our own voice is shaped and changed by the anatomy of our own head. But when others hear us, we do sound much like that unfamiliar voice emanating from the recorder. Reality and perception can be quite different.

This is why it's one thing to ask you if you're a patient person, and it's quite something else to ask others whether or not you're patient.

What would your spouse say if asked whether you are a patient person? Your children? Your friends? Fellow workers? Employees or employer? Fellow church members? The answers might surprise you.

Some folks readily admit to being impatient. They'll warn you, "I have a temper." Then they'll justify it by explaining, "I'm Irish," or "Hey, it's my red hair," or "I had a bad day at the office." They're telling us "I have a foul disposition and you just have to lump it."

But why should I have to accept that in you? Why should you have to tolerate that in me?

"It's just the way I am"!

Isn't that the lamest excuse you ever heard from someone wanting to be like Jesus? A central tenet of the Christian faith is that with the Lord's help we can be changed. If we shrug our shoulders at our impatience and justify ourselves, we are actually trying to hide a defect behind a flimsy excuse. Instead, we should expose our shortcoming in a spirit of penitence to the power of God that works in us (Ephesians 3:21).

It's wise to recognize your impatience, but it is foolish to insist that you can do nothing about it. Impatience, anger, and a lack of steadfastness can cost dearly—your happiness, that of others, even your soul.

Just how patient are we? Can we wait for things to happen on their own good schedule, or are we so impatient for them to happen that we try to hasten them? Impatience is often our greatest enemy, because it makes us so restless that we spoil the very thing we are seeking to attain.

A person is not born with patience. I wasn't, and I'm pretty sure you weren't either. It is something we must learn. A baby is a terribly impatient creature. We have that old saying about something being "as easy as taking candy from a baby." Did you ever try taking something from a baby? Easy it ain't! You may get it from the baby, but there are loud consequences to contend with.

It is a mark of immaturity and impatience when a person cannot wait for the greater goals of life and insists on being satisfied with lesser ones. As a rule, a child would rather have a quarter right now than wait for a five dollar bill next Monday.

Patience is definitely an acquired taste, a product of God's working in us. Paul tells the Galatian Christians that " . . . the fruit of the Spirit is love, joy, peace, patience, kindness, goodness, faithfulness, gentleness and self-control. Against such things there is no law" (Galatians 5:22, 23). Patient people pick a sweet fruit.

People have said to me, "You are the most patient person I've ever known." Usually my response is a simple "Thank You." Inwardly, I'm thinking "Patience, my foot!" I know that they haven't seen all of me. The degree of patience which I'm able to display at this stage of dealing with my disability is not a static quantity. It used to be considerably less, and the level varies even yet—and always will. But it's as if people believe that polio produces patience. The misconception applies to all disabilities, illnesses, and misfortunes. People act as if the card for patience were dealt in the same hand with misfortune. I'm here to tell you that "It ain't necessarily so."

The Greek origin of our word "patience" implies two ideas: perseverance and endurance. It can mean either a willingness to wait, or continuance in our effort to achieve. Both of these elements should be present in our lives. It's like having moxie, chutzpah, grit.

Who wants patience anyway? And why? We all need this virtue, in varying degrees, because when we possess it we can live in greater peace—no matter what circumstances come our way. "The fear of the LORD leads to life: Then one rests content, untouched by trouble" (Proverbs 19:23).

Let's explore some ways to develop and strengthen this thing called patience, which Chrysystom called "The Queen of the Virtues." Remember, if you want it, then patience is only a matter of time.

CHAPTER 2
There Are No Curtain Calls

Welcome to Greek 101. Actually, I've never studied Greek at all. And you are probably in that same canoe with me. What I know about the Bible's Greek roots is all second hand. However, that's okay if you select reputable, qualified Bible scholars to depend on. They spend their lives getting a handle on the significance of ancient Greek in order to shed more light on Scripture's exact meanings.

Great. But what does that have to do with being patient? Hang in there. We will see the biblical basis for this habit of patience.

Scripture obviously promotes the notion of patience among God's people.

"Be still before the LORD and wait patiently for him; do not fret when men succeed in their ways, when they carry out their wicked schemes" (Psalm 37:7).

"The end of a matter is better than its beginning, and patience is better than pride" (Ecclesiastes 7:8).

"The Lord direct your heart into the patience of Christ" (2

Thessalonians 3:5 Amplified Bible).

Talking about patience makes me a little nervous. Sometimes I have a problem with being patient. I like to plant and harvest the same day. And I think that this attitude of "I want what I want when I want it" is universal. Otherwise, how could you explain the marvel of fast food eateries? They are not such successes because the food is a gourmet's delight. Fast food thrives because it is fast—and we are impatient creatures.

Paul prayed for his brethren that "The Lord direct your hearts into the patience of Christ." This is a prayer all of us would do well to make our own: "The Lord direct my heart into the patience of Christ."

The Bible emphasizes again and again the importance of patience. "Be joyful in hope, patient in affliction, faithful in prayer" (Romans 12:12). "Love is patient, love is kind . . . " (1 Corinthians. 13:4). "But the fruit of the Spirit is love, joy, peace, patience, kindness, goodness, faithfulness" (Galatians 5:22). "By standing firm you will gain life" (Luke 21:19). Or, as the King James Version renders it, "In your patience possess ye your souls."

A lot of passages urge us to patience. But what is it? Patience is a biblical word still in circulation. Many words of the King James era are no longer in common use, or their meanings have changed. If I were to tell you that "Last week I was in such sore straits I was pricked in my reins," you'd think I was crazy. But that phrase is just good Old English which means "Last week I was worried sick." The word patience, however, is still used, and it still carries the same meaning.

The word translated "patience" in the text of Galatians 5:22-23 is *makrothumia*. Thayer defines it as " . . . endurance, constancy, steadfastness, perseverance; especially as shown in bearing troubles and ills" (Greek-English Lexicon, page 387).

A Greek synonym for *makrothumia* is *hupomone*, a noun usually translated "patience" in the New Testament. Thayer's definition of this word says, "In the N.T. the characteristic of a man who is unswerved from his deliberate purpose and his loyalty to the faith and piety by even the greatest trials and sufferings" (Thayer, page 644).

In his *Analytical Greek Lexicon* (page 418), Bagster defines *hupomone* as "Patient endurance, patient awaiting, a patient frame of mind, patience, perseverance, endurance in adherence to an object." This word appears in verses such as these: "But the seed on good soil stands for those with a noble and good heart, who hear the word, retain it, and by *persevering* produce a crop" (Luke 8:15). "Not only so, but we also rejoice in our sufferings, because we know that suffering produces *perseverance*; perseverance, character; and character, hope" (Romans 5:3,4). "For this very reason, make every effort to add to your faith goodness; and to goodness, knowledge; and to knowledge, self- control; and to self-control, perseverance; and to *perseverance*, godliness" (2 Peter 1:5,6). There are many other Bible references highlighting this Greek word *hupomone.*

Recently I was reading a brief but inspiring biography of Thomas Edison written by his son. What an amazing man! Thanks to his genius, we enjoy the incandescent light, the microphone, the phonograph, the storage battery, talking movies and more than a thousand other inventions. But beyond all that, Edison was a man who had learned to deal with his own adversity and disability (he was hearing impaired)—and refused to be discouraged. His contagious optimism affected all those around him.

His son told about a freezing December night in 1914. Unproductive experiments on the nickel-iron-alkaline storage battery, a 10-year project, had put Edison in a tight financial bind. The only thing keeping him solvent were the profits from movie and record production.

On that December evening the cry "Fire!" echoed through the laboratory. Spontaneous combustion had ignited reels of movies in the film room. Within minutes all the packing compounds, celluloid for phonograph records, film, and other flammable goods were burning. Fire companies from eight surrounding towns fought the blaze, but the heat was so intense and the water pressure so low that attempts to extinguish the flames were futile. Everything was being destroyed.

When he couldn't find his father, the son became concerned. Was he safe? With all his assets being destroyed, would his spirit be broken? Soon he saw his father in the yard running toward him.

"Where's Mom?" shouted the inventor. "Go get her, son! Tell her to hurry up and bring her friends! They'll never see a fire like this again!"

Early the next morning, long before dawn, with the fire barely under control, Edison called his employees together and made an incredible announcement. "We're rebuilding," he said.

He told one man to lease all the machine shops in the area. He told another to get a wrecking crane from the Erie Railroad Company. Then, almost as an afterthought, he added, "Oh, by the way, anybody know where we can get some money?"

Later, he explained, "We can always make capital out of a disaster. We've just cleared out a bunch of old rubbish. We'll build bigger and better on the ruins." Shortly after that, he yawned, rolled up his coat for a pillow, curled up on a table and immediately fell asleep.

That, as Thayer defines patience, is real " . . . endurance, constancy, steadfastness, perseverance; especially as shown in bearing troubles and ills." Edison knew what it was about.

Thayer also adds that patience includes elements of " . . . Forbearance, long suffering, slowness in avenging wrongs." It is the endurance of wrong without anger or retaliation. The person who is patient will bear with the weaknesses of others. That person will have his temper under control and will be able to endure insult and injustice. This patience is not merely a shallow good nature, but is a fruit of the Spirit that makes for love and peace and enables one to bear injury without taking vengeance.

Makrothumia is used in the Septuagint (the ancient Greek translation of the Old Testament) to translate a Hebrew phrase meaning "slow to anger": "The Lord is slow to anger, abounding in love and forgiving sin and rebellion" (Numbers 14:18a).

I'm sure grateful that the Lord isn't short fused. If He were an impatient God, He would have torn up my contract long ago. He has had to be patient with me far beyond the limit to which I would have gone for someone else. I think of that familiar passage: "The Lord is not slow in keeping his promise, as some understand slowness. He is patient with you, not wanting anyone to perish, but everyone to come to repentance" (2 Peter 3:9). It isn't that God does not take notice of our wrongs. He just reacts differently to provocation than we do. God is waiting with restraint. He gives us time to respond properly to life and to Him. In His dealings with us, God demonstrates loving endurance, constancy, steadfastness, perseverance, forbearance, long suffering, and slowness in avenging wrongs—in a word, patience.

Isn't that the basis of our need to exercise patience? We sing a hymn about "I love the Lord because He first loved me." Well, we must be patient too, because of His great patience with us.

God usually works in His natural world with steady leisureliness. He has no need to hurry, because He is not confined by time. Jesus, in His earthly ministry, demonstrated this same method of working. I am sure that the patience of Jairus was severely tested when Jesus was journeying to his home to heal his sick daughter. Jesus even stopped along the way to help others. But He says to Jairus, "Fear not, only believe."

Many things can test our patience. In a situation like that of Jairus the Ruler, we could become impatient when we see others procrastinating and causing discomfort or harm to our loved ones. Or a long period of illness and disability can be very trying. That's when folks often get irritable and bored, because time moves so ponderously when we are impatient. The ten minutes that an impatient parent must spend waiting for a child to come out from school can seem like an hour.

Vaughn Monroe, a popular singer in the 1940s and 50s, observed, "This would be a fine world if men showed as much patience all the time as they do while they are waiting for a fish to bite."

It sometimes seems as though the little frustrations are the ones that try us most severely. We can fly off the handle so quickly when we are provoked, especially if the provocation hits us close to home. There are annoyances in the home, or at work, or even while driving down the highway, that can cause us to lose our temper. A can of sardines won't open, a nail bends under the blows of our hammer, or a golf ball finds the nearest sand trap instead of the green, and our patience is strained. Sound familiar?

We may even blame the objects or persons that frustrate us. I remember when I was a kid I loved building plastic models. Doing it with the toes of one foot is not the same as using two hands. However, I got quite good at this skill. Besides the usual cars, airplanes, and rockets, I also built many HO scale model railroad cars and structures. My favorite kit was a Swift meat packing facility for my model railroad layout. It was a wood, cardboard, and diecast metal assemblage—no pre-formed pieces to just glue in place. Components had to be measured out and cut from sheets of heavy cardboard or strips of balsa wood. It was a real challenge—for any hobbyist. At one point, I remember getting so aggravated at a perverse piece which would not fit where it was supposed to fit that I kicked the whole thing halfway across my room. Frustration can do that. My outburst achieved nothing—except to undo a lot of what I'd worked hard to accomplish. The real problem was not in the pieces of that kit, nor in my X-Acto knife, nor the glue I was using. I know it, and you know it: the real problem was within me. I had to learn to conquer my own nature. And it's a never- ending struggle. But it's vital if we are to learn the art of patience. When things have gone wrong a dozen times, patience says "I can do it again."

Two cousins of mine, Jessica and Jay, when they were ages six and four, had been enjoying a video of *Sleeping Beauty* which their mom had rented. Jessica was enamored with the prince and the princess of this fairy tale. She acted out the scenes again and again, compelling brother Jay to play the part of the handsome prince. As Jessica lay dramatically in state on the landing of their stairway, Jay would awaken her with a princely kiss. But he had gone along with the story line about as many times as he could tolerate. Enough is enough, after all. So when Jessica directed him to play the role again, Jay stiffened his back, shook his finger sternly, and announced, "One more time, Jessie, one more time."

Even in a four-year-old, that is a great display of patience. We need to develop that inner resource which, even in severe distress, can summon the strength to pray "One more time."

When your patience is fraying and you're about to give

vent to it, what should you do? Think about God's patience. "Bear in mind that our Lord's patience means salvation . . . " (2 Peter 3:15). We have benefited from God's patience far in excess of our own small opportunities to react with patience.

Life is like a three act play: You're born, you live, and you die (that's euphemistically called "curtains," an appropriate theatrical term, don't you think?). Consider it. You've already been born—that's Act One. You've lived—that's Act Two. How long till Act Three? Remember, you're never too young to die. Act Three is always at hand, and there are no encores.

Don't take this reality in the wrong way, however. It isn't a morbid idea. But it should add perspective to life. In the theater, actors wait in a place called the green room for their cues to go on stage. For a child of God, this life on earth is just the "green room" for the big show that is yet to debut. But for the unbeliever or for the person in rebellion to God's will, this life is it. "What you see is what you get." "It doesn't get any better than this." "Eat, drink, and be merry, for tomorrow we die."

And how does that relate to patience? The outlooks of the "Material Person" and the "Forever Person" have everything to do with ultimate and true patience. The "Material Person" must grab for the gusto—quick, because when it's time for Act Three . . . boom . . . down comes the curtain. There isn't even time for a final bow. If that's your fate, you can't be very patient with anything or anybody that gets in the path of your headlong rush to maximum satisfaction before it's time for the reviews to come in. Isn't that a mini portrait of the age we live in?

But what if your personality is focused on "forever"? In that case, with your eye on eternity, you understand that you're just passing through this dirty theater on your way home. In the language of the Bible, we're just pilgrims and strangers here. So the annoyances we encounter, whether major or minor, are just that—annoyances. They are the training exercises to equip us for a future we can only imagine.

CHAPTER 3

"I'll Pay Back the Three Zillion Bucks I Owe You"

God's patience and our own are remarkably unalike. Do you remember Jesus' parable about "The Unmerciful Servant"? It could as easily be titled "The Parable of the Impatient Servant."

Therefore, the kingdom of heaven is like a king who wanted to settle accounts with his servants. As he began the settlement, a man who owed him ten thousand talents was brought to him. Since he was not able to pay, the master ordered that he and his wife and his children and all that he had be sold to repay the debt. The servant fell on his knees before him. "Be patient with me," he begged, "and I will pay back everything." The servant's master took pity on him, canceled the debt and let him go. But when that servant went out, he found one of his fellow servants who owed him a hundred denarii. He grabbed him and began to choke him. "Pay back what you owe me!" he demanded. His fellow servant fell to his knees and begged him, "Be patient with me, and I will pay you back." But he refused. Instead, he went off and had the man thrown into prison until he could pay the debt. When the other servants saw what had happened, they were greatly distressed and went and told their master everything that had happened. Then the master called the servant in. "You wicked servant," he said, "I canceled all that debt of yours because you begged me to. Shouldn't you have had mercy on your fellow servant just as I had on you?" In anger his master turned him over to the jailers to be tortured, until he should pay back all he owed. This is how my heavenly Father will treat each of you unless you forgive your brother from your heart (Matthew 18:23-35).

We're talking real shekels, pesos, pounds sterling in the case of the first servant. It is difficult to figure out the exact value of the ancient "talent." Some authorities say that a talent was equal to fifteen years' wages of a laborer, while a "denarius" was a day's wages for a laborer. Maybe it's hopeless to try to calculate the precise dollar values of these debts, but the real point is as plain as the nose on your face: the debt of the first guy is a fabulous sum equivalent to tens of millions of dollars. This fellow owes ten thousand talents. To put that in perspective, Josephus, the ancient historian, reports that the total taxes for Judea, Idumea, and Samaria for one year were only six hundred talents, and those of Galilee and Perea were just two hundred. This man had been living the good life on a credit card and had run up a tab of ten thousand talents, with each talent being worth fifteen years' wages. You do the math—that's 10,000 times 15. A mere 150,000 years of labor would take care of this debt.

The debt of the second servant, on the other hand, is equal to about one hundred days' wages. That's a manageable sum. "Easy terms available." Notice that the first servant implored the king, "Be patient with me." Then he was approached by the man who owed him a paltry sum by comparison, and his fellow servant also begged "Be patient with me." Though the first servant had asked the king for and had been granted patience—a cancellation of his hopeless debt—he refused to show patience to another. He was justly condemned because of his unforgiving and thankless heart. "'This is how my heavenly Father will treat each of you unless you forgive your brother from your heart,'" warned Jesus (Matthew 18:35).

That's scary. If God has been patient with you, how dare

you not show patience to others? Divine and human patience go hand in hand *quid pro quo*. If you know that God has been patient with you, you should certainly be willing to be patient with someone else. When we consider God's "slowness to anger," it hardly seems appropriate for us to have a short fuse and to blow up in impatience with others—mate, children, parents, employees, brethren, or whoever. Unless we are patient and merciful, God will eventually withhold His patience and mercy from us. His promise is not vain and we will reap what we sow.

Patience is a child of faith. Bret Harte wrote of a gold miner in California who dug his claim vigorously until he decided there was no gold to be had there. So he sold his claim "dirt cheap." The man who bought the claim discovered a rich vein of gold. Why did the man who sold too soon remain poor when he might have been rich? He lost faith in his claim and then he lost his *patience*.

God made Abraham a promise that in his seed all nations would be blessed. Abraham never lost faith in God's promise. Even when Abraham was 100 years old and Sarah was 90, he still believed God and patiently waited for the promise to be fulfilled. Abraham's power to wait patiently was born of his great faith.

Have you noticed? Some people just won't be stopped. Like Abraham, they have accomplished much despite adversity. They refuse to listen to their fears and doubts or to give in to their impatience. Nothing anyone says or does holds them back. As Ted Engstrom insightfully writes in his book *Pursuit of Excellence*:

> Cripple him, and you have a Sir Walter Scott. Lock him in a prison cell, and you have a John Bunyan. Bury him in the snows of Valley Forge, and you have a George Washington. Raise him in abject poverty and you have an Abraham Lincoln. Strike him down with infantile paralysis, and he

becomes Franklin Roosevelt. Burn him so severely that the doctors say he'll never walk again, and you have a Glenn Cunningham—who set the world's one-mile record in 1934. Deafen him and you have a Ludwig von Beethoven. Have him or her born black in a society filled with racial discrimination, and you have a Booker T. Washington, a Marian Anderson, a George Washington Carver . . . . Call him a slow learner, "retarded," and write him off as uneducable, and you have an Albert Einstein.

Patience is a child of love. "Across the years I have seen marriages pulled out of the fire by patience born of love," says my dad, James, a gospel preacher for more than fifty years.

What makes a mother patient with her duties in the home—exacting and endless as they are? What enables my mother, Jackie, to deal with my care, a grown son, plus the responsibility of her own mother who is mentally disabled by old age, and to carry on her own life as well? It is the patience of love. What made Jacob patient enough to toil fourteen years for Rachel? It was love.

Patience is also the product of hope. We endure afflictions, remain steadfast at duty, labor against opposition, because of our hope of immortal glory. "In my father's house are many mansions . . . ," said Jesus. That should build hope and patience.

This is the kind of hope that must have lived in Joseph and Jeremiah, two Old Testament characters who could have said "Life is the pits"—figuratively and literally. But instead, they were patient with the role set before them.

You remember Joseph's story in Genesis. His jealous brothers sold him into slavery, telling their father, Jacob, that his favorite son had been killed by wild beasts. Joseph ended up as a servant in the home of a high Egyptian official. Joseph was a man of considerable faith, love, and hope, because instead of anger and resentment he invested himself in dedication to the task before him. His faithful service, in what could have been unhappy circumstances, elevated Joseph to a level in Egypt second only to Pharoah. Through God-given wisdom, Joseph took charge of Egyptian agriculture and internal affairs to stockpile food for the days of famine he knew were coming. In time, the drought and hunger drove his own family from Canaan to Egypt in search of food. Joseph's hope for reunion with his father and brothers was realized. His patient endurance of a life in servitude had rewarded him at last. When the brothers learned that this powerful Egyptian ruler was actually their little lost brother Joseph—who they sold to slave traders—they were rightfully scared out of their sandals.

All those years had passed, and Joseph could have been fretting and fuming over this injustice wrought against him by his no-good brothers. When their father, Jacob, died, the brothers' fear surfaced again. They worried that with Jacob gone Joseph would feel free to retaliate.

> So they sent word to Joseph, saying, "Your father left these instructions before he died: 'This is what you are to say to Joseph: I ask you to forgive your brothers the sins and the wrongs they committed in treating you so badly.' Now please forgive the sins of the servants of the God of your father." When their message came to him, Joseph wept. His brothers then came and threw themselves down before him. "We are your slaves," they said. But Joseph said to them, "Don't be afraid. Am I in the place of God? You intended to harm me, but God intended it for good to accomplish what is now being done, the saving of many lives. So then, don't be afraid. I will provide for you and your children." And he reassured them and spoke kindly to them (Genesis 50:16-21).

Joseph chose the better way, the patient way, the way of love and hope. He faithfully saw to the task given him and awaited what God had in store.

Jeremiah was another guy who found himself in a pit. He was God's prophet to Judah, beginning his ministry to the nation about halfway through the reign of King Josiah (640-609 B.C.). The people had once again forsaken Jehovah and gone into idolatry for the umpteenth time—even to the degree of murdering their own children on the altars of Baal. But the Living God was preparing to send Judah into captivity in order to cleanse the people. Jeremiah, the weeping prophet, was to call the nation back to righteousness, warning them that resistance to the invading Babylonians would cause death and destruction. Only submission to God's will—to captivity—would bring salvation. Jeremiah loved the people, despite their sins, and prayed for them continually—even when the Lord said not to (Jeremiah 7:16; 11:14; 14:11).

And how did the people react to Jeremiah's intercession on their behalf?

They said, "Come, let's make plans against Jeremiah; for the teaching of the law by the priest will not be lost, nor will counsel from the wise, nor the word from the prophets. So come, let's attack him with our tongues and pay no attention to anything he says" (Jeremiah 18:18).

"Should good be repaid with evil?" prayed the prophet. "Yet they have dug a pit for me. Remember that I stood before you and spoke in their behalf to turn your wrath away from them" (Jeremiah 18:20).

The powers who ruled Judah had decided that they'd heard enough. Jeremiah was upsetting their apple cart with his gloom and doom preaching. They would, as Archie Bunker used to say, "Stifle it." They threw him in a dry well to let him die. But Jeremiah lived to see that what the Lord revealed through him came to pass. Read Jeremiah 38 to hear all of this remarkable story. The prophet was patient and true to his duty, and God was true to His word.

"I have my rights!" That's the screech we hear bellowed across America these days. The attitude is "I want what's mine—and I want it now." David, the boy who would be king of Israel, was selected by the Lord himself to take over the kingdom from Saul. David was God-ordained to rule the nation, and he knew it.

> So he [the prophet Samuel] sent and had him [David] brought in. He was ruddy, with a fine appearance and hand-some features. Then the LORD said, "Rise and anoint him; he is the one." So Samuel took the horn of oil and anointed him in the presence of his brothers, and from that day on the Spirit of the LORD came upon David in power (1 Samuel 16:12, 13).

Did David "demand his rights"? Was David impatient and contemptuous with Saul—who God had chosen David to replace?

"David came to Saul and entered his service. Saul liked him very much, and David became one of his armor-bearers. Then Saul sent word to Jesse, saying, 'Allow David to remain in my service, for I am pleased with him . . . '" (1 Samuel 16:21-23).

"Jonathan [Saul's son] spoke well of David to Saul his father and said to him, 'Let not the king do wrong to his servant David; he has not wronged you, and what he has done has benefited you greatly'" (1 Samuel 19:4).

David was patient and waited for God to make him king at the proper time. David trusted the Lord's scheduling of things. He didn't try to rush events, or to destroy the insanely insecure Saul—or even to taunt Saul with the inevitable. David waited for the Lord's time to come. And not only did he wait, he also ministered kindly to Saul, who was trying to kill him.

In time, David succeeded Saul as king of Israel and under

his rule the Lord prospered the nation, defeated its enemies, and fulfilled His promise (see Genesis 15:18) to expand its borders from Egypt to the Euphrates (2 Samuel, chapter 8). David wanted to build a temple for the Lord—a royal residence for the true King of Israel. It would be a magnificent place to house the throne of God himself (the ark of the covenant). It would be a place for Israel to worship the Lord.

That sounds good, doesn't it? It was a worthy ambition on the part of David. But the prophet Nathan informed David that he would not be allowed to build the Lord's house because of "bloody hands" from his many wars. Instead, the Lord would build a great house (a dynasty) from David, would bring forth a son to build the temple, and ultimately would provide the victory over the evil one through David's descendent—the Christ (2 Samuel 7).

And the temple began to rise in the reign of Solomon, David's son, who contracted for materials with King Hiram of Lebanon:

> "You know that because of the wars waged against my father David from all sides, he could not build a temple for the Name of the LORD his God until the LORD put his enemies under his feet. But now the LORD my God has given me rest on every side, and there is no adversary or disaster. I intend, therefore, to build a temple for the Name of the LORD my God, as the LORD told my father David, when he said, 'Your son whom I will put on the throne in your place will build the temple for my Name.' "So give orders that cedars of Lebanon be cut for me. My men will work with yours, and I will pay you for your men whatever wages you set. You know that we have no one so skilled in felling timber as the Sidonians." When Hiram heard Solomon's message, he was greatly pleased and said, "Praise be to the LORD today, for he has given David a wise son to rule over this great nation" (1 Kings 5:3-7).

David patiently accepted God's decree. He was even joyful

in the fact that others would, in fact, construct the temple for the Lord. He was excited about the idea, whether he could do it or not. No wonder David was known as a man after God's own heart.

There are good reasons why David was unhasty and why he should be restrained in his actions. David was forgiven by the Lord time after time, including the incident of adultery and murder involving Bathsheba. David realized the tremendous debt he owed God because of the Lord's great patience with him.

Did you ever think about the patience of Mary, the Lord's mother? Her patience and endurance are admirable above all other women in the Bible. Think of the honor and pride she must have felt at being the mother of the Messiah. Nothing in all the universe could compare with the reality of being mother to the Savior of the world. Like every mother, Mary must have felt an unusual pride in her special son when the wise men from the East—and even the angels from heaven—paid homage to her child. But her heart must have ached in heaviness when she had to endure seeing and hearing the scorn and ridicule heaped upon her son.

The most ghastly test of her patient endurance, and the heaviest of her heartaches came when she witnessed her son's suffering on the cross. And imagine how triumphant her joy must have been when the angel at his tomb proclaimed, "He is not here; he has risen, just as he said. Come and see the place where he lay" (Matthew 28:6). Mary's patience, her faith, her endurance carried her through to the divine confirmation of the Sonship of Jesus, who was Christ the Lord.

While Abraham, Jeremiah, David, Mary, and other Bible characters are helpful examples of patience for us to observe and emulate, our perfect example of patience is the Lord Jesus Christ. Peter tells us, "To this you were called, because Christ suffered for you, leaving you an example, that you should follow in his steps" (1 Peter 2:21).

Did you ever try to learn the art of calligraphy? You perfect the skill by copying and practicing elements of the letters of the alphabet. You learn how to hold the pen, then you go through the motions again and again while keeping an eye on the patterns in the instruction book. You trace and copy and follow the examples. This is the same image that Peter sketches for us. The word translated "example" in 1 Peter 2:21 is *hypogrammos*, the line of writing which a schoolchild copies—a pattern for making letters and words. Jesus is the Word which we imitate, and He inspires and leads us as He speaks to us through His written word, the Bible. The indwelling Spirit shows the Christian the things of Christ as revealed to the writers of the New Testament: "But the Counselor, the Holy Spirit, whom the Father will send in my name, will teach you all things and will remind you of everything I have said to you" (John 14:26). "But when he, the Spirit of truth, comes, he will guide you into all truth. He will not speak on his own; he will speak only what he hears, and he will tell you what is yet to come. He will bring glory to me by taking from what is mine and making it known to you" (John 16:13-14).

Jesus is the trailblazer for our faith and patience. "Let us fix our eyes on Jesus, the author ["trailblazer"] and perfecter of our faith, who for the joy set before him endured the cross, scorning its shame, and sat down at the right hand of the throne of God" (Hebrews 12:2). In the same way that the wagon trains headed west by following the trail blazed by their scout, the Christian can develop the self-discipline of patience by following the example of Jesus. "As children copy their fathers you, as God's children, are to copy him," Paul wrote to the Christians at Ephesus (Ephesians 5:1 Phillips).

Christ is the perfect exemplification of the fruits of the Spirit described in Galatians 5. Paul exhorts us to follow the Lord's superb example of love: "and live a life of love, just as Christ loved us and gave himself up for us as a fragrant offering and sacrifice to God" (Ephesians 5:2).

Likewise, the writer of Hebrews, as we saw a minute ago, urges "Let us fix our eyes on Jesus, the author ["trailblazer"] and perfecter of our faith, who for the joy set before him endured the cross . . . " (Hebrews 12:2). The word translated "fix our eyes on" is very strong in the Greek. It conveys the idea of giving our undivided attention—looking away from everything else. The verse imparts the image of discipline in place of distraction. One of the powerful lessons we can learn from the example of Jesus is that a right motivation for disciplined endurance of suffering is the promise of joy.

The fruit of peace is so closely allied with the nature of Christ that it is impossible to separate the two thoughts. He is the very "Prince of Peace" (Isaiah 9:6), an attribute prophesied nearly eight hundred years before His birth. When He was born, angels proclaimed "peace on earth" (Luke 2:14).

Christ is also the perfect manifestation of the Spirit's fruit of patience. Paul says, "But for that very reason I was shown mercy so that in me, the worst of sinners, Christ Jesus might display his unlimited patience as an example for those who would believe on him . . . " (1 Timothy 1:16).

Jesus embodies flawless goodness—even in the face of malevolent circumstances, showing us self-control over circumstances and surroundings.

And Jesus is the perfect example of faithfulness. He was faithful to the Father, to His role as Redeemer of humanity through His own death, to His promises, and even to His unbelieving people—all in spite of the antagonism and anxiety generated by Satan and his cohorts. "He was faithful to the one who appointed him . . . " (Hebrews 3:2). "The one who calls you is faithful and he will do it" (1 Thessalonians 5:24). " . . . he will remain faithful, for he cannot disown himself" (2 Timothy 2:13).

If it weren't for the faithfulness of Christ, how could we even hope to sustain our own self-discipline? "But the Lord is faithful, and he will strengthen and protect you from the evil one" (2 Thessalonians 3:3).

We must be patient if we are to be like our Lord. This, after all, is the purpose of our religion—to bring us ever increasingly to a likeness of the Lord, who is patient. In describing the Lord's dealings with unfaithful Israel in the wilderness, the prophet Nehemiah says,

> They refused to listen and failed to remember the miracles you performed among them. They became stiff-necked and in their rebellion appointed a leader in order to return to their slavery. But you are a forgiving God, gracious and compassionate, slow to anger and abounding in love (Nehemiah 9:17).

In the New Testament, we learn from the pen of Peter that " . . . God waited patiently in the days of Noah while the ark was being built . . . " (1 Peter 3:20).

"The Lord is not slow in keeping his promise, as some understand slowness. He is patient with you, not wanting anyone to perish, but everyone to come to repentance" (2 Peter 3:9).

We are commanded to be patient. God expects it of His people. "Be still before the LORD and wait patiently for him" (Psalm 37:7). "Be joyful in hope, patient in affliction, faithful in prayer," Paul writes to the Christians in Rome (Romans 12:12).

The fruits of the Spirit, or graces, are not isolated skills. They are interrelated, working together, supporting each other in our struggle to produce self-control—and patience.

CHAPTER 4

Patience, Patience Everywhere

Lots of folks concede that patience is a handy trait for the sick, disabled, and incarcerated. After all, those kinds of people really need to be patient. Right?

Let me assure you that patience is not a virtue to be practiced only by the ailing, the disabled, and those in the hoosegow. Because in all of life each of us must learn to practice patience. I don't know of many other qualities of the soul that are more important for personal peace.

Patience is not a genetic inheritance. None of us is born with a developed capacity for exercising patience. It is something we must learn—and practice. A baby is one of the most impatient creatures under the sun. Just observe how long a hungry baby is willing to wait for its milk. It is characteristic that the immature person cannot wait for a greater goal in life and insists on possessing a lesser one—right now.

In *Tough Times Never Last, But Tough People Do!*, Robert Schuller wrote of a woman who emigrated from Mexico to the United States with her husband and children. On their way to "paradise" in the United States, at the border in El Paso, Texas, her husband deserted her, leaving her stranded with

43

the children. A divorcee, twenty-two years of age with two kids, she was poverty-stricken. With the few dollars in her pocket, she bought bus tickets to California. She was sure that she could find work there. And she did find a job—an awful job, working from midnight until six o'clock in the morning, making tacos. She earned only a few dollars, but she ate meagerly and saved a dime from every dollar she earned.

Why did she struggle to save when her own needs and those of her children were so desperate? She saved because she was visualizing a dream—she wanted to own a taco shop. One day she took the few dollars she'd managed to save, went to a banker, and said, "There's a little place I'd like to buy. If you'd loan me a few thousand dollars, I can have my own taco shop."

The banker, impressed by her, decided to take a chance and loaned her the money. She was twenty-five years old and the owner of a little taco shop. She worked hard at it, and eventually, she expanded and expanded until today she has the largest wholesale business of Mexican products in America. She also went on to become the treasurer of the United States. Her name is Ramona Banuelos.

She demonstrated the characteristics of a mature person who can postpone immediate gratification in favor of a greater, longterm goal.

All worthwhile accomplishments require some amount of time to achieve. When you plant a seed in your garden you must wait for the sun and the rain and the nutrients of the soil to work their magic. Any attempt on your part to hurry up the process will hinder the growth—or kill the plant. You cannot change the natural rhythm of life, and you cannot force things too far out of their present shape without doing some damage.

There's an old Dutch proverb which says, "A handful of patience is worth more than a bushel of brains."

The patience and self-discipline of Christ are personified in His incarnation. This same humility and self-discipline need to be developed in our own lives. Paul writes about it. He says,

> Your attitude should be the same as that of Christ Jesus: Who, being in very nature God, did not consider equality with God something to be grasped, but made himself nothing, taking the very nature of a servant, being made in human likeness. And being found in appearance as a man, he humbled himself and became obedient to death—even death on a cross! (Philippians 2:5-8).

Jesus "humbled himself." Take note of the six attributes involved in this self-discipline.

First, He willingly (as a matter of His mind and will) set aside His rights, His birthright, His prerogatives. It required great self-discipline, sacrifice—and patience to do that. But shouldn't we be willing—as a matter of our own mind and will—to surrender our agenda and to exercise patience to His glory? After all, "A student is not above his teacher, nor a servant above his master" (Matthew 10:24). We don't deserve better than the Lord Himself. And Paul advises us to "Submit to one another out of reverence for Christ" (Ephesians 5:21). If that's not a call to patience, I don't know what could be.

This whole concept of "submission" to others—a basis for patience—sounds strange to our ears. Our minds can barely envision it. We have "rights."

"How dare that driver stall his car in front of me?"

"You're supposed to be home for dinner at 6 o'clock—sharp."

"That sales clerk can't keep me waiting like this. I'm gonna let her know it too."

"I've been a member of this church for twenty-five years and I deserve . . . ."

"I want what's coming to me."

Have you ever noticed that sometimes we get impatient, angry, and remain bitter with people and actually forget why we're so upset? Take the example of the notorious Hatfield-McCoy feud.

It first hit newspaper front pages in the 1880s, when the Hatfield family feuded with the McCoy clan from across the border in Kentucky. Historians disagree on what started the feud—which captured the imagination of the nation during a 10-year course. Some cite Civil War tensions: McCoys sympathized with the Union, Hatfields with the Confederacy. Others say the feud began when the McCoys blamed the Hatfields for stealing hogs. As many as 100 men, women and children died from what probably began as anger between two anonymous individuals.

This tragedy had an agreeable ending. In May 1976, Jim McCoy and Willis Hatfield—the last two survivors of the original families—shook hands at a public ceremony dedicating a monument to six of the victims.

McCoy died Feb. 11, 1984, at age 99. He bore no grudges— and had his burial handled by the Hatfield Funeral Home in Toler, Kentucky.

Second, Jesus had the power to do otherwise, but He chose to "make himself nothing." He wasn't preoccupied with His image in humanity's mind. He didn't fret, "I can't be a servant; people won't respect me as God that way."

Third, Jesus submitted to the Father's wishes and took on the form of a slave. Submission and servitude always require self-discipline. That's probably why most of us aren't over-joyed with the prospect of servanthood. Jesus excelled at His servanthood through inner strength, actuated by a vision of future joy, by His love for the Father, and by His dedication to redeeming our souls.

Fourth, He condescended, He chose to lower Himself in the order of things and to take on the likeness of human kind. He was accustomed to the heavenly hierarchy: God, Christ, the Spirit, and angels. But He allowed Himself to be made human. As the psalmist tells it, "You made him a little lower than the heavenly beings [angels]" (Psalm 8:5). This gave Him full insight into our human frailties, "For we do not have a high priest who is unable to sympathize with our weaknesses, but we have one who has been tempted in every way, just as we are—yet was without sin" (Hebrews 4:15).

The fifth and sixth attributes of Christ's self-discipline and patience revolve around His death. He not only chose to die, but He also allowed that death to come by way of a humiliating and excruciating means. The pure, righteous, and holy Son of God allowed us to see Him tortured to death as a common, corrupt criminal.

He could have chosen to avoid human death altogether. He could have chosen to die peacefully as an old man. He could have ascended back to the Father at the transfiguration. But instead He chose the way of submission and endurance. He *decided* to accept an accursed death (Galatians 3:13).

I can hear it now: "We can't exert the degree of will, self-discipline, and patience that Jesus did—we're only human, He is divine." Granted, we can't control ourselves that way through our own strength and efforts. We just don't have what it takes in our human condition. But don't forget or discount the promise Jesus made to His obedient followers: "He will do even greater things than these, because I am going to the Father" (John 14:12). After He ascended to the Father, the Comforter came to indwell believers. "When the Counselor comes, whom I will send to you from the Father, the Spirit of truth who goes out from the Father, he will testify about me" (John 15:26).

We have access to the same empowering Spirit who guided Christ into His great self-discipline and patience. "And if the Spirit of him who raised Jesus from the dead is living in you, he who raised Christ from the dead will also give life to your mortal bodies through his Spirit, who lives in you" (Romans 8:11). Through the Spirit and the Word that he has revealed, we can access the enabling power of Heaven.

There is a word for grace in your New Testament. That word is *charis*. It is what empowers us to transform outward circumstances from unpleasant to acceptable—and even beneficial. That's the power by which Christ transformed death into life, disaster into triumph, and disorder into order. It was not a task that came to fruition without patience. And the same Father who empowered His patience is there for us today.

Jesus embodied perfect self-discipline and patience in all aspects of His life. He was disciplined mentally, physically, emotionally, socially, and spiritually. Here's how Luke described Jesus at the age of twelve: "And Jesus grew in wisdom [mentally] and stature [physically], and in favor [emotionally] with God [spiritually] and men [socially]" (Luke 2:52).

Patience is a need of our physical body. Jesus exercised great patience in training his body physically through the discipline of fasting. On one occasion He fasted forty days and nights (Matthew 4:2). He taught His disciples its benefits (Matthew 17:21, Mark 9:29).

The three recorded temptations of Christ included testing of His patience in controlling His physical nature. Remember? When He was famished after fasting in the desert, Satan tried to get Him to turn stones into bread—a temptation to get "right now" what He had the power to get, rather than to wait for food in due time. The response of Jesus is a key for us in opening the door to patience: the spiritual always takes priority over the physical. The eternal always comes before things that are worldly. Natural, legitimate physical needs, such as hunger, sex, companionship, the need for money, must be satisfied in God's way and on God's own schedule.

In the second temptation, Satan suggested to Jesus that He test the Father's promise of protection by jumping from the high pinnacle of the temple. Jesus rebuked this idea too. Even though He had the right to expect such protection, Jesus did not demand a demonstration of God's protective hand.

The third temptation was the most beguiling, because it was a temptation to do wrong (yield to Satan) for the right reason (reclaim the world for God). Satan appealed to Christ to take an impatient shortcut by bowing down to him instead of following the road to the cross and its anguish.

Things haven't changed much. Satan still says "be impatient to fulfill your physical desires"; be impatient and insist that your way is God's way—and presume on His protection no matter what your actions; and be impatient about enduring discomfort (whether it be physical, emotional, or spiritual).

Only self-disciplined patience and reliance on God's Word will bring us to victory. That's how Jesus, our example, won it.

Patience is a need of our emotions. Jesus was altogether God and altogether man (a concept that still makes my head spin when I try to comprehend it), but as all-God and all-man He was tempted in every way that we are tempted—but He never yielded to a temptation to sin (Hebrews 4:15). He experienced every form of human emotion without losing control. His great love never deteriorated into indulgent sentimentality or blinded Him to truth.

Jesus delighted in doing the Father's will (Psalms 40:8), and in fulfilling the law of God (Psalm 119). Through grace and the exercise of patience, He found joy and purpose in enduring the pain and shame of the cross.

We often make the mistake of underestimating the torment, the desperate urge to impatience, and the emotional emptiness which Jesus dealt with in Gethsemene (Matthew 26:37-38; Mark 14:33-34). But He did not give in to anguish. He was not overcome by it. Instead, He made the conscious decision to submit to the Father's will and to endure what followed that decision. Jesus was

> . . . despised and rejected by men, a man of sorrows, and familiar with suffering. Like one from whom men hide their faces he was despised, and we esteemed him not. Surely he took up our infirmities and carried our sorrows, yet we considered him stricken by God, smitten by him, and afflicted (Isaiah 53:3-4).

But it was our grief He bore, our sorrows that weighed Him down. He cried for Jerusalem (Luke 19:41-44), and he wept when Lazarus died (John 11:35). But somehow Jesus never lost the balance between sadness and joy, between anguish and enjoyment, between depression and exultation. He never did allow Himself to be assigned to the ranks of the downhearted and defeated. Instead, He always identified Himself as the joyful and victorious One.

Jesus could show concern, but He was never distracted by worry or anxiety. He lived a disciplined life that set Him free to be real and relaxed because of His total trust in the Father. "Foxes have holes and birds of the air have nests, but the Son of Man has no place to lay his head," said Jesus (Matthew 8:20). He had a "philosophy" of life and He lived by it:

> "Therefore I tell you, do not worry about your life, what you will eat or drink; or about your body, what you will wear. Is not life more important than food, and the body more important than clothes? Look at the birds of the air; they do not sow or reap or store away in barns, and yet your heavenly Father feeds them. Are you not much more valuable than they? Who of you by worrying can add a single hour to his life? And why do you worry about clothes? See how the lilies of the field grow. They do not labor or spin. Yet I tell you that not even Solomon in all his splendor was dressed like one of these. If that is how God clothes the grass of the field, which is here today and tomorrow is thrown into the fire, will he not much more clothe you, O you of little faith? So do not worry, saying, 'What shall we eat?' or 'What shall we drink?' or 'What shall we wear?' For the pagans run after all these things, and your heavenly Father knows that you need them. But seek first his kingdom and his righteousness, and all these things will be given to you as well. Therefore do not worry about tomorrow, for tomorrow will worry about itself. Each day has enough trouble of its own" (Matthew 6:25-34).

Learning patience does not mean that you never feel anger. However, "righteous indignation" is rarely the same as our human anger. Jesus became angry without sinning. "In your anger do not sin: Do not let the sun go down while you are still angry . . . ," the apostle Paul advises (Ephesians 4:26).

In clearing the temple of the greedy, unprincipled money-changers, Jesus personified "righteous indignation," taking time to braid a whip and driving out the animals and merchandisers (John 2:13-16). Our problem is in letting impatience gain the upper hand, and then we rename ugly, vengeful loss of temper as "holy wrath." Jesus became angry when evil men violated the sanctity of His Father's House—not when men abused Him. We, on the other hand, tend to lose control when we are personally affronted, rather than when God is offended. Christ's anger was legitimate; ours is rarely so. He showed that we can't love as we should unless we also know what and how to hate.

I haven't personally checked this out, and I'm not going to, but I have heard that when a rattlesnake is cornered, it can become so frenzied it will accidentally bite itself with its deadly fangs.

In the same way, when we harbor hatred and resentment, we are hurt by the poison of our own malice. We think we are injuring our enemies by displaying our wrath, but the real harm is inflicted deep within our own soul.

Anger can also cause us to do and say things we may deeply regret. George W. Martin tells the following true story:

> I remember a fellow who once wrote a nasty letter to his father. Since we worked in the same office, I advised him not to send it because it was written in a fit of temper. But he sealed it and asked me to put it in the mail. Instead, I simply slipped it into my pocket and kept it until the next day. The following morning he arrived at the office looking very worried. "George," he said, "I wish I had never sent that note to my dad yesterday. It hurts me deeply, and I know it will break his heart when he reads it. I'd give 50 dollars to get it back!" Taking the envelope from my pocket, I handed it to him and told him what I had done. He was so overjoyed that he actually wanted to pay me the 50 dollars!

Jesus was physically and verbally attacked, but His response to this was always with love, forbearance, and restraint. Look at His reactions: "I offered my back to those who beat me, my cheeks to those who pulled out my beard; I did not hide my face from mocking and spitting" (Isaiah 50:6). As the song says, "He could have called ten thousand angels," but He chose to act with patient self-control.

Do you remember that scene in the garden when Jesus rebuked Peter for lopping off the ear of the high priest's servant? Jesus told Peter that He could have called down those twelve legions of angels to protect Himself. But He didn't. Instead, He did good to one who meant Him harm. This is also our goal, to "Bless those who persecute you; bless and do not curse . . . Do not be overcome by evil, but overcome evil with good" (Romans 12:14, 21). This kind of patience to endure abuse in the face of blatant mistreatment is not a trait of "the natural man." But it is a real possibility for those who have been born into the kingdom of the dear Son of God, who is our perfect model and our enabler.

Patience is a need for our social self. No matter what our station in life might be, we need to submit to the will of others from time to time, a requirement calling for the exercise of patient forbearance. Again, Jesus is our living, breathing, and perfect pattern. As a child, He was submissive to Joseph and Mary. "Then he went down to Nazareth with them and was obedient to them" (Luke 2:51). He was subject to civil authorities and taught His disciples to "Give to Caesar what is Caesar's, and to God what is God's" (Matthew 22:21).

Patience is a need of our spiritual self. Jesus exemplified the ideal and had every right to hold it up in front of us for an image of how we should be. "By myself," He said, "I can do nothing; I judge only as I hear, and my judgment is just, for I seek not to please myself but him who sent me" (John 5:30). Submission to the Father's will was not a burdensome task for Jesus. It was His reason for living. "'Here I am—it is written about me in the scroll—I have come to do your will, O God'" (Hebrews 10:7).

During Jesus' thirty-three years of earthly life, He showed us a pattern for the patient and purposeful use of time. His example was one of "making the most of every opportunity, because the days are evil" (Ephesians 5:16). "Be wise in the way you act toward outsiders; make the most of every opportunity" (Colossians 4:5). We never saw Jesus in a breathless rush or flying off in every direction at one time, and yet He never seemed to be late. He was always in proper synchronization with life around Him. When He got the message that His friend Lazarus was seriously ill, He waited two days before going to him. Mary and Martha were understandably disturbed and scolded Jesus, saying if He had come "in time" their brother would still be alive (John 11:21, 32). But Jesus showed them that the only yardstick for a patient and purposeful use of time is "that God's Son may be glorified through it" (John 11:4).

In submitting to the Father's will, and "As the time approached for him to be taken up to heaven, Jesus resolutely set out for Jerusalem" (Luke 9:51). He gave us an unequaled example of self-control and patient peacefulness in the face of dreadful circumstances. "Hallelujah, What a Savior"!

To comprehend His patience, listen to His silences. It's hard to stay silent when you are personally mistreated and provoked. But under the barrage of lies coming from the chief priests and the elders, and under Pilate's interrogation Jesus spoke not a word (Matthew 27:12-14). When He did speak, everyone knew that "No one ever spoke the way this man does" (John 7:46). His responses were reasoned, wise, and full of grace.

Amazingly, the enemies of Jesus assumed that His fate was in their hands, and yet He was the one in control of the flow of events. No one took His life—He chose to forfeit His life on His own terms. "The reason my Father loves me is that I lay down my life—only to take it up again. No one takes it from me, but I lay it down of my own accord. I have authority to lay it down and authority to take it up again," He told His disciples (John 10:17-18). In our own lives, it can seem that evil, or circumstances, or other people are ruling our destiny, but if we patiently submit to His will for us we can come to the point where we see another hand guiding and holding us up.

You can learn to discipline your body and your will to some extent, but until you have a spirit that's disciplined by the Spirit your efforts will accomplish little of lasting significance. Unless you get in touch and stay in touch with the Word of the Lord, you'll never be able to develop the self-control needed for becoming truly patient. You can read self-help books, listen to self-improvement tapes, and attend "take charge of your life" seminars—and you'll gain some measure of self-improvement—but these humanistic do-it-yourself techniques are doomed to failure because they ignore the all-important realm of the spiritual. As you might suspect, Jesus was again our perfect model. He knew that the ability to deal patiently with life grew from deep wells of inner strength. So "very early in the morning, while it was still dark, Jesus got up, left the house and went off to a solitary place, where he prayed" (Mark 1:35). Later Jesus sent the disciples away while He went up to the mountain to pray. And Luke tells us that Jesus went into the hills and prayed all night (6:12).

Jesus is our model of self-discipline and patience. But then Satan reminds us that Jesus was God, and we're merely frail humans—we are destined to fail. Let's admit it: that is all true—as far as it goes. We *will* fail if we rely on fleshly strength to support spiritual aims. But we can claim the same reservoir of strength which Jesus depended on. We must submit to it, intimately know its will, and commune with it—as He did—and then we can tap into strength for our earthly task. As God, Jesus could not fail. As a human, He was empowered so that He need not fail. That's our salvation. Energized by the Word of the Spirit, we too can be empowered in living so that we need not fail to be what we seek to become in the Lord.

CHAPTER 5

Patience Is Like a Trip to the Toy Store

When my brother and sister and I were young, Dad would occasionally be away from home for a week preaching a revival meeting somewhere out of town. The family would on rare instances all go along. But it's awkward to deal with three young children away from home for a busy week's worth of preaching, studying, and so on. That's why Mom and we kids usually stayed at home. This was especially the case after I had polio. We could—and did—haul my respirator and other special requirements on trips, but we liked to pick and choose, since travel was a particular adventure.

Since we were left at home while Dad was away, he formed a tradition of bringing everybody a "surprise" each time he came home. If he had not had time while away, or if he couldn't find an appropriate homecoming present, then he might take us to the toy store to select our own surprise. Naturally, this was an anticipated treat. We were given an upper limit on the cost, but beyond that, anything in the store could be ours!

Two stores were our treasure troves. When you couldn't find something at one, then the other was sure to come through. The first was a neighborhood Ben Franklin "dime store" of the type you can't find anymore. It was operated by Mr. and Mrs. Martin. He went to church where we did, and she was a good Baptist lady. Going to Ben Franklin's was like a visit to your grandma's house—only better!

The second store we relished visiting was Uncle Lee's Toy World. It was a old-style toy store, very different from the modern shopping mall stuff. It was owned and operated by a man who was "Uncle Lee" to every kid in town. Wonderful places, both of them.

Well, one Monday afternoon, when Dad had returned from an out of town trip, he took us shopping. We looked at everything in Ben Franklin's, but you know how it is. We were afraid that we might miss something, so we begged to go check out Uncle Lee's before making up our minds. Then it was another hour's worth of looking for just the right surprise.

My sister, Loris, and I found our most wanted items pretty quickly, but Kevin, our five-year-old brother, was really struggling to make up his mind. Dad was ready to go home, Loris and I were ready to go home, but Kevin was still befuddled by all his options. My granddad used to say that it was cruel to take a kid to a toy store, and he may have been right.

Well, Kevin did make up his mind. He selected a Dinky Toy scale model Army Jeep. But the point of the tale isn't what toy Kevin got. Rather, the thing that has made this one of our favorite family stories is Kevin's comment year's later: "If for no other reason," he said, "I'd know that Dad loved me because of that trip to Uncle Lee's. Everybody was ready to go home, but I couldn't make up my mind what to buy. I can still see Dad sitting on a box, resting his head on his hand and telling me 'Take your time, son, take your time.' That's love."

And that's patience, of the sort that's sorely needed in

families. My two nieces and my nephew each got in the
school band when they got to middle school. Jaima Beth, the
oldest, took up the French horn; Marla studied the flute; and
Ryan took the trumpet. They all spent a lot of time at our
house, so Mom, Dad, and I got to listen to a big share of their
practice time. Do you know how much you must love a child
to endure his or her learning to play the French horn? Or the
flute? Or the trumpet? You do if you've been there. It's
patience personified. It makes me appreciate my parents
more for the two years I took piano lessons beginning at age
six.

Patience at home is a valuable commodity these days.
You're responsible for your own patience quotient, so how
do you measure up? What would your spouse say if asked
whether you are a patient person? Your children? Your parents? Your siblings?

We have to begin by being patient with ourselves. "By
standing firm you will gain life" (Luke 21:19). "Standing firm"
is another way of saying "steadfast." We need to hang in
there and not go to pieces. Our spiritual maturing takes time.
"Therefore, rid yourselves of all malice and all deceit,
hypocrisy, envy, and slander of every kind. Like newborn
babies, crave pure spiritual milk, so that by it you may grow
up in your salvation, now that you have tasted that the Lord
is good" (1 Peter 2:1-3). It may take a hundred years for an
acorn to produce a mighty oak. And it takes time to grow a
mature soul too—a lifetime.

Husbands and wives should guard against an unreal expec-
tation of perfection from each other; otherwise, impatience is
inevitable. And today's insistence on individual rights, rather
than on mutual submission to the overriding will of God, cre-
ates all sorts of problems. Submission and patience are closely related concepts.

My mother, Jackie, has lived a life of patience—being a

preacher's wife. If you've never been on the inside of a preacher's family, you can't really imagine what it's like. He's your father, or he's your husband—but he's THEIR preacher.

Maybe it's your birthday, and you've planned a family event—but then the phone rings. That brother or sister in the congregation who has been critically ill for weeks has suddenly died, and the preacher has to go. Or a church member has a personal or family crisis and needs to talk to the preacher right now—even if he is your dad or your husband. And it's not that you really resent such interruptions of your life, but it does call for patience. I have no idea of how many times Mother kept supper warm for Dad until he came home from a Bible class, elders' meeting, counseling session, and a thousand other events in the daily routine of a preacher. And I wish I had a nickel for every time Mother said, "We won't wait for Daddy to get home tonight, so let's go ahead and eat now." Patience was and is a daily requirement in her life.

Parents can avoid many clashes with children if they'll maintain realistic and understanding expectations.

> O! Give me patience when little hands
> Tug at me with ceaseless small demands.
> O! Give me gentle words and smiling eyes,
> And keep my lips from hasty, sharp replies.
> Let me not in weariness, confusion, or noise,
> Obscure my vision from life's few fleeting joys.
> Then when in years to come, my house is still,
> No bitter memories its rooms may fill.
>
> — author unknown

Patience is truly a precious possession in a home where an elderly mother or father, or grandmother or grandfather is living. They move *slower*. They relive the past—again and again. They repeat and repeat. Every word spoken to them must be repeated once, twice, three times. They answer your phone and tell an important business caller that you don't live there. Because of them, schedules and activities must be rearranged. All of this presents you with occasions to develop patience in ways you never before imagined. But we need this patience at home.

How about outside your home? What would your friends say about your level of patience? Fellow workers? Employees or employer? Fellow church members? The answers might surprise you.

We need patience in telling others about the Lord. "You can send a message around the world in one-seventh of a second," said C.F. Kettering, "yet it may take years to force an idea through a quarter-inch of human skull." Patience is called for in teaching the gospel (1 Timothy 3:3; 2 Timothy 4:2; Hebrews 13:17). How many times have you heard it when someone comes to the Lord?—somebody will say, "I've been waiting and praying for years for this." It takes exhorting, praying, teaching, showing, pleading, and loving—and being quiet, to bring a life to Christ, or to reclaim one who has wandered away. It takes time.

Patient or impatient?—these questions can give you a clue:

Do you hastily retaliate when wronged?

Can you bear with unpleasant people and circumstances until a right solution is found?

Are you long-suffering even in adversity?

Do you have a degree of tolerance even for the intolerable?

Do you try to understand the awkward people or disturbing events that God allows to enter your life? "A patient man has great understanding, but a quick-tempered man displays folly" (Proverbs 14:29).

Do you persevere and produce positive results even under opposition and suffering?

Are you able to forgive someone as often as he or she asks for it?

Do you drink instant coffee and eat a lot of microwave dinners?

Do you often eat in fast food restaurants?

Do you attend seminars, buy tapes, and read books on "How to Have Success—Right Now"?

Are you short tempered, especially with your own family? "Better a patient man than a warrior, a man who controls his temper than one who takes a city" (Proverbs 16:32).

Do you find that you usually answer people in kind—harsh word for harsh word, blow for blow, eye for eye and tooth for tooth?

Do you expect adult behavior from your children when they are actually incapable of such at their present level of maturity? Do you patiently let them grow out of their immaturity?

How do you measure up under these situations?

When your husband dawdles and dinner is on the table, getting cold?

When you are sitting in the car with the engine running and she is still putting the finishing touches on her make-up?

When you need the telephone and the daughter is lying

across her bed, feet on the wall, talking to some unknown entity—and has been for 30 minutes?

Can you wait without losing your cool when your order at the restaurant is delayed long after those of others who came in after you did?

Do you become increasingly resentful when the amen to a prayer or end of a sermon is delayed long beyond what you thought it should be?

Can you wait and hope with a breaking heart that someone you love will overcome an evil, self-destructive behavior?

These are the times when we must figuratively and literally "count to ten"—and most important of all, turn our impatience over to the Lord in a spirit of penitence so that His power can work in us (Ephesians 3:21). The time to react is NOT when the heat of impatience is firing up. That's why the old "Count Ten" adage has some validity. Judgment is a whole bunch clearer if your mouth isn't full of scalding hot coffee. Once you get a scalding hot mouthful, you're going to spew it without much thinking or looking.

How do you react when your husband makes a social obligation for the evening you'd bought expensive tickets to a concert; or your wife makes a social obligation for the night you'd bought high-dollar tickets to a basketball game; one of your employees fails to recognize the importance of a call from your most prized client, and now you could lose the account because that client is upset at not receiving the attention he expects; one of your cars is in the shop, your teenager takes the other car to the mall and assures you that he will be back in time for you to make that important appointment at lunch—but he isn't, because he and his buddies let time get away from them.

The urge to kill! Anger and impatience seem to be standard equipment for us humans. To be angry, or not to be angry is not the choice. The question is "How will I deal with my impatience and anger?"

Anger and hostility are by-products of living in today's world—for employees and employers, spouses, in-laws, even children. And where you find anger, you find impatience. You generally want to mask anger, especially if it would cause you to lose your job, or to get a fist in the mouth. But covering up impatience doesn't save you from all damage. Medical experts say that anger causes physiological changes such as a red face, increased heart rate, raised blood pressure, surging stomach acid, even impotence, and a definite desire to punch out somebody's lights. They warn us that anger can be just plain unhealthy. It affects our performance and success in all areas of life.

Allowing impatience to lead to runaway anger is like using dynamite to get rid of ants in the kitchen. It results in actions that are out of proportion to reality.

Keith Hendricks (not his real name) has wrestled with a temper all his life. When his wife was late getting home from work recently, he sizzled with every tick of the clock. His imagination ran wild. He thought she was spending money. No, she was with a man. No, she was deliberately delaying in order to irritate him. Keith's anger worked his imagination overtime. In reality it was his wife who was working overtime. Her employer asked her to finish a report before a holiday vacation. She was only forty-five minutes later than usual, but Keith was so worked up that when his wife came in the door he yelled, cursed, slammed his fist through a wall, and broke his own hand in the process. That's the wages of impatience.

Al Slaton, a former felon with a string of arrests ranging from armed robbery to murder, has rehabilitated his life. He built a career as a nursing assistant in a VA hospital in Texas. On the side, he provided food and shelter to disabled vets and street people with nowhere to go. Welfare agencies were unable to serve these people. They were the folks who have "fallen through the cracks" of the system. The problem is acute for persons with mental diseases. Hospitals will keep them only a short time and then release them back to the streets. The "lucky" ones went to prison. The more Al tried to find help for these people, the more he felt as though he were butting his head against a stone wall. He became angry with "the system." So he opened a halfway house to care for schizophrenics, the homeless, and others in need of this kind of supervision. Anger was channeled into action.

Some situations which make us angry are susceptible to remedies. If a wife is upset because her husband is always late to supper she can serve it at a later hour, she can persuade him to get home earlier, he can prepare his own meal, or they can eat out at whatever time he gets home. She doesn't simply have to live with hostile emotions, because there are options.

But dealing with anger and frustration in healthy ways becomes vital when the offending situation cannot be changed. Patience takes on added significance when there are no alternatives. "I wonder what other disabled people do to release anger, (and) frustration...," a recent letter asked readers of *Accent on Living*, a magazine for physically challenged people. I can assure you that those of us with disabilities deal with added frustrations in life, and the cause of that frustration—the disability—in most cases is not going away. And all of us experience stresses in life that are not going away.

Since most of us don't know effective techniques for dealing with anger, we instinctively resort to our own inner devices. Some folks use a stiff drink for numbing their rage. And you know the effect that alcohol has on a fire. Drugs—both prescription and illegal varieties—are another dead-end approach. Or we may try to squash angry feelings and then end up paying the physical price that suppressed fury can exact. We react as we have learned to react. We are products of our training. Fortunately—and thank God—we are still trainable, even those folks with severe impatience problems.

"Very little study has been done on normal behavior," says Dr. Herbert A. Schubert, a friend and a psychiatrist recently retired from the Veterans Administration. "Most study has been done on pathological cases. There has been more emphasis on how things go wrong than there has been on why things go right. But most people do take disaster and make something useful out of it."

Our impatience, like dynamite, has useful applications. We can channel the energy of this emotion to build something positive when we are faced with obstacles.

Anger and impatience are natural emotions. Temper, on the other hand, is a learned behavior. We become angry naturally, but we learn what to do with anger by watching our role models and from experimentation. Your techniques for dealing with anger are major personality shapers. Your typical level of anger affects how you perceive yourself and others, and it determines how you'll cope with stress.

When you feel helpless, frustrated, or inferior, temper may flare to protect your psyche. Temper is a common defense mechanism. The more insecure and vulnerable you feel, the more intense your anger.

And anger, while it can be a strong motivator, is still essentially a negative, self-centered emotion. But people who are not self-oriented, whose interests are focused outward towards others, tend to possess more positive attitudes toward life. People who follow the Lord's example of seeking opportunities to do good for others will find little time or room in their heart for impatience and anger.

A problem identified is a problem on the way to being

solved. What makes you angry?

Here's a list that should help you understand the areas where you're vulnerable: do your feathers get ruffled at being rebuffed; being ignored; being cheated; getting patronized; feeling like others control your life; being defied; suffering slander or gossip; being bossed around; being humiliated; not being able to complete plans and activities; being rebuked by an inferior; being lied to; being disappointed in what you expected from others; seeing your family or others mistreated; being dependent; getting the holier-than-thou treatment; enduring ridicule; facing condescension; or being misunderstood. All of these work for me!

But someone has said, the truest test of moral courage is the ability to ignore the insult.

So the question is "What will you do with your anger?" Impatience is always easier to fall into than to get out of. Alibis won't cut the mustard. We must control anger if we're to live peacefully and successfully. "Be angry and sin not," says the Bible.

Unfortunately, temper infuses a sense of power when we're feeling vulnerable. A blistering temper is exhilarating. It's an adrenaline high. However, temper addicts can end up with a hangover of headache, fatigue, nausea, and even black-outs. Guilt feelings also go along with temper outbursts.

You can't enjoy productive, pleasant relationships if you vent your anger. It must be controlled, and that doesn't mean bottling it up—which can result in all sorts of unpleasantness. But the need to sometimes express anger doesn't give you license to scream, curse, and kick the dog any time you're annoyed.

Folk wisdom says to "get it out of your system." Jack Nicklaus says he still bends a golf club around a tree now and then, but he makes sure nobody sees it and that he uses an old club which he won't need again. Generally, flying off the handle in a rage will only alienate people. This is particularly true on the job. Carol Tavris, in her book *Anger: The Misunderstood Emotion*, says that people who tend to vent their anger also tend to get more angry more often. Showing your anger might make you feel better, but the effect is short lived and it alienates those around you. A better approach is learning internal techniques for dissipating anger.

The first lesson to learn is that frustrations aren't going away—but you can learn to deal with them in more satisfying ways, according to my friend Dr. Schubert. We can't redirect the wind, but we can adjust our sails.

Instead of fretting, fuming, and exploding, can you somehow make anger work for you?

Begin by accepting responsibility for your own impatience and anger. You may feel uncomfortable with that, but it's necessary. No one can ever make you angry unless you first give them permission. You must allow it to happen. There's nothing intrinsic to any "provocation" which triggers a reflex in us to "be mad." Anger itself is a natural emotion. But the list of our own personal trip levers is under our control—particularly as it relates to our response to an anger stimulus. To understand your own struggles with impatience, focus on the situation, on the factors that triggered your anger response. Then remind yourself that your anger is unproductive and will only lead to more problems. See if the response can't be delayed for thirty minutes. You'll be amazed at how many situations will simply evaporate when deliberately postponed.

Now and then you may still find yourself grinding your teeth and ready for a fight. If so, maintain control. Inhale deeply, slowly. Practice building a habit of self-control in place of temper. Imagine a pleasant aroma—a fragrant rose or a cheery fire in the fireplace. As soon as possible after a run-in with someone, do something you really enjoy. Play golf, go biking, play tennis, go to the lake, eat a piece of chocolate. Distract your mind so that you'll know there's more to life than just this present aggravation. Remember, impatience gnaws at a person's life like a moth eating away at a wool blanket.

Once you've calmed down, take Dr. Schubert's advice and "turn disaster into something useful." Nothing quiets impatience like service to others. Focus on a goal and task. Concentrate on what you want to come out of this situation. Do you want to save the relationship with that other person? With the goal in mind, decide what needs to be done now.

A matter-of-fact confrontation may be required in order to iron out details for avoiding future problems. In *Values Clarification*, authors Sidney Simon, Leland Howe, and Howard Kirschenbaum suggest confronting people with *RDAs*. First, tell the person you're angry with what you Resent: "I'm annoyed that you chose to miss that meeting this morning." Then express your Demand: "I want you to be at the follow-up meeting tomorrow morning." Finally, express something positive you Appreciate about the person: "I always rely on your input because you have a good handle on this situation."

Once your anger is under control and the situation is calm, it's wise to consider some preventive medicine for short circuiting future problems.

Examine your expectations of yourself and of others. Are you unrealistic? Are you inflexible? If so, you're setting the stage for inevitable conflicts, impatience, and anger.

A successful young businessman said, "I have learned that it pays to have a high expectancy of good. So many people expect the worst. Perhaps things do look black, but why expect a storm? Why not expect the sun to break through?

Why not expect the best to happen? There is something magnetic in the way one thinks."

Be aware of the situations which trigger your temper, and when they arise let a little red flag in your brain signal DANGER. During calm moments, imagine yourself in aggravating situations, and then envision how to handle them with serene self-assurance. Use these mental images for internal role patterns.

Put the other person in the best possible light. Try to understand and sympathize with the pressures and demands on him or her which pushed them into the situation.

If you find yourself frequently in stressful situations leading to angry encounters, whether on the job, at home, at church, in school, or wherever, look for ways to ease those day-to-day tensions. Join a health club, develop a hobby. Eat lunch out more often. Make friends on the job who share your experiences, because misery really does love company.

Quit being resigned to just absorbing your frustrations. Keep expressing your expectations in positive ways. Even if they're not met, you'll feel better for having voiced them.

The future is not inevitable, you know? We have choices. We're always coming to new forks in the road. God is more concerned with your responses to a problem than He is with removing the problem. Paul said,

> To keep me from becoming conceited because of these surpassingly great revelations, there was given me a thorn in my flesh, a messenger of Satan, to torment me. Three times I pleaded with the Lord to take it away from me. But he said to me, "My grace is sufficient for you, for my power is made perfect in weakness." Therefore I will boast all the more gladly about my weaknesses, so that Christ's power may rest on me (2 Corinthians 12:7-9).

Good manners are a social grace that has nearly disappeared from our culture. When impatience flares, the average person can do more harm with his mouth than with a gun. So when you are at a loss for the right word to say, try silence. No one is too big to be courteous, but some are too small.

Above all, strive to be honest about your feelings. Whether it's in your role as spouse, parent, child, church member, church leader, boss, employee, club member, or citizen, do all that's in your power to keep communications open and flowing. It will keep anger in its proper perspective.

You cannot maintain noble desires, aspirations, and ideals unless the root that connects them with the Source is intact. Elton Trueblood reminded us of this in his instructive book, *The Predicament of Modern Man*. He says that Christian ideals become only cut flowers and soon wither away if they are severed from their life-giving roots. The brotherhood of man has no real meaning apart from the fatherhood of God.

Only as we give allegiance to God through Christ can we be safe in risking our desires and the desires of other men.

When Jesus said, "Lay up for yourselves treasures in heaven," he did not mean that we are to get busy trying to pile up in heaven the things we treasure on earth, but rather we are to learn to treasure the things of heaven. Hunger and thirst after righteousness. Learn to treasure, to love, to delight in heavenly things. Yearn for goodness, strive for purity, hunger for patience—and our reward will be according to our desires.

We can't learn to cherish the things of heaven until we come to know the King of heaven. Getting to know Him, trying to understand His will, attempting to do His will—only this will help us learn to desire the things and the ways of heaven. When such a relationship between us and God predominates in our lives, then and then only are we safe and successful in the exercise of our self-improvement efforts.

Every success at taming your impatience will enable you to win future victories. If you do regress now and then, and you find yourself slamming doors too vigorously, don't give up on yourself. You're only human. Just back up, take a deep, slow breath, say a prayer, and resolve that next time you'll deal with your anger in a mannerly way.

CHAPTER 6
Get Ready for Spring Training

The "boys of summer" became the men of October in a very special way in 1991. Even the Commissioner of baseball said that this was probably the greatest World Series ever. For the first time in history, two teams went from last place in their respective divisions to league champions. When all seven games of the World Series had been played, four games had been settled by the last player who batted. Players on both sides played their best under the strain and pressure generated by millions of fans watching their every move.

John York, the preacher at my home congregation, lived in Atlanta for three years and has been a die-hard Braves fan through many bad seasons. He would take his two young sons to the games. "It was always easy to get seats to watch them lose another one," he says.

Yet, every spring brought promises and hope for a brighter day, a better year, a competitive team. "But it never took very long for the hope to fade and the losing to become commonplace," says John. After he moved away from Atlanta, he says "I stopped subscribing to cable TV in part so that I wouldn't agonize over 'America's Team' losing day after day."

But the 1991 season was different. The last place team suddenly was challenging for first place. The Braves won their division and then came back to win the league championship. Then they came back from a 2-0 deficit in the World Series to actually lead three games to two. The last two games both went into extra innings before Minnesota won them and the championship. Even though Minnesota took home the trophy, there were no losers in the 1991 series. Over 500,000 people filled the streets of Atlanta to pay tribute to their team when it came home. The last became first, and it was a great day to celebrate.

Baseball is just a game. To some people, it's a slow, boring game. It is a distraction from the real world where we all live. We love to see losers become winners because it allows us to share the fantasy of being winners ourselves. So we wish for a fairy tale reversal in our own lives.

But baseball players aren't suddenly ready for the World Series just because the calendar turns from September to October. Warm ups for October's World Series begin with spring training in March. Diligent preparation is the secret.

It's all based on perseverance, keeping on keeping on. But there are two forms of perseverance: one is as the world knows how to persevere (and that can be inspiring, as in the case of sport), and there is perseverance in the Lord—which will be redemptive in every way.

"If anyone is to go into captivity, into captivity he will go. If anyone is to be killed with the sword, with the sword he will be killed. This calls for patient endurance and faithfulness on the part of the saints" (Revelation 13:10). Later in the book, the apostle John says again, "This calls for patient endurance on the part of the saints who obey God's commandments and remain faithful to Jesus" (Revelation 14:12).

The apostle is talking about the church's enduring persecutions, but the truth that he expresses also applies to our enduring what Trine Starnes, the late gospel preacher, liked to call "the vicissitudes of life."

Some people think of sports as trivial wasters of time and money. And in the eternal scheme of things I guess sports don't possess much real importance. Yet I find that sport can be an instructive and inspiring microcosm of "real life."

An article in the July/August 1989 issue of *Success Magazine* relates the experience of Michael J. Coles, for whom every day has become an exercise in patience and an opportunity for a comeback.

A catastrophic motorcycle accident taught him the most important lesson of his life: You must always surpass your goals.

Life was sweet when Coles and a partner launched the Original Great American Chocolate Chip Cookie Co. with $8,000. In the first month, his company pulled in $32,000. Then it happened.

"I was on my way home on my motorcycle," recalls Coles. "I hit a rock and slammed into a telephone pole." He regained consciousness the next morning in the hospital. With three limbs in casts and his face wrapped in bandages, he slowly set about rehabilitating his body and his business.

Coles made what others considered to be acceptable progress. One day, however, he was limping up his driveway when his daughter challenged him to a race. He tried to run, and then he froze. "I realized I was mentally handicapped, too."

Stung by shame, Coles took his first real step forward: "I decided that moment that whatever it took I would try to fully recover." He devised a painful rehabilitation regimen of weight lifting, squatting, and bicycling. "I set an impossible goal: I would become the best bicyclist around."

After four years of training, he bicycled across the country in fifteen and a half days—a new world record. But all Coles could think about was breaking his own record. And he did it two years later.

Coles also pushed an aggressive franchise plan that has now reached sales of $70 million. "The accident taught me something," Coles says. "If you get run off the road, you get right up and start over again." That's purpose. That's perseverance. That's patience.

Vince Lombardi, the legendary coach of the Green Bay Packers, made a film in which he drums this never-say-die principle into the heads of football players. The film is titled *Second Effort*. It motivates players to do more than memorize plays, train faithfully, and work hard. It urges them to keep going when everything within them cries out "Stop." He incites them to pick up the extra necessary yards after they have already been hit and tackled.

That's purpose. That's perseverance. That's patience.

That's also the philosophy employed by a well-known community college coach in Fullerton, California, whose thirty-five-plus years in athletics have been eminently successful.

Hal Sherbeck grew up in big-sky country and became a winning coach at Missoula High School. This led to a coaching career at the University of Montana, where he distinguished himself with an enviable win-loss record. Ultimately, Sherbeck went to California, where he has been coaching at Fullerton Community College for many years. His extraordinary career in Southern California speaks for itself. When he was interviewed by the *Los Angeles Times*, the sportswriter asked his secret. What was it that made him so successful?

Without hesitation Coach Sherbeck said that his credo could best be stated in words written by an anonymous author. Ever since he was a boy growing up in Big Sandy, Montana, he has lived by these words:

Press on.
Nothing in the world
Can take the place of persistence.
Talent will not;
Nothing is more common
Than unsuccessful men
With talent.
Genius will not;
Unrewarded genius
Is almost a proverb.
Education will not;
The world is full of
Educated derelicts.
Persistence and determination
Alone are important.

Coach Sherbeck had no quick and easy formula for success; he lives by his strong commitment to persistence and determination.

Calvin Peete grew up in central Florida's farm country, where he and his family made a living picking vegetables. Like any other young person, Calvin had dreams. But considering his background, Calvin's dream seemed far-fetched: he wanted to be a professional golfer. His friends laughed at him, because poor blacks just didn't become professional golfers.

In the eighth grade, Calvin had to drop out of school and go into the fields to help his family earn a living. But, despite his daily labor, he always felt that God intended more for him than picking vegetables all his life. His dream of becoming a professional golfer would not roll over and die, and Calvin took up the game as an adult.

You talk about disadvantages—Calvin not only began golf at a late age, but he had to play with a left arm that wouldn't fully straighten out as a result of a broken elbow when he was a child. Professional golfers would say it's impossible to play golf without an extended left arm. But Calvin compensated for that disability, and within six months he was shooting below 80. Within another eighteen months, he was shooting below par and joined the mini-tour in Florida in 1972. Then in 1975, he qualified for the PGA tour—the oldest rookie in history, at age 35. He won the Greater Milwaukee Open in 1979, and again in 1982, when he became the winningest golfer on the tour. Calvin's persistent belief that God has a plan for his life empowered him to persevere without giving up.

Calvin said in an interview in *Plus Magazine* in 1989:

It's been a long road from the fields to the fairways, one a lot of people said was impossible. But you see, I knew something maybe they didn't. That God had a plan for me—but I had to be willing to work at it. When you work hard and pray hard, you have a combination that can take you places you've never imagined. It's taken me from green beans to a putting green . . . and far, far beyond.

That's purpose. That's perseverance. That's patience.

Wilma Rudolph had polio as a child. The disease left her with a crooked left leg. She wore metal braces and had to have treatments for over six years. At age 11, through sheer diligence and determination, she made herself walk without braces for the first time. Her older sister was a good runner, and at age 12, Wilma started to think about running. What a decision. She then started acting on her decision to be a runner. She talked to the coach and asked for a special time.

He said, "I'll give it to you, Wilma."

In two years, she outran all of the other girls in her high school in Clarksville, Tennessee. Two years later, in 1956, she ran in the Olympics in Melbourne, Australia, and won the bronze medal. Four years later, in 1960, in Rome, she was ready. She had paid the price. She won, and she won big. She won the 100 meter dash. She won the 200 meter dash. She anchored the United States relay team and won three gold medals. A young, disabled black girl reached for the gold—and grasped it.

That's purpose. That's perseverance. That's patience.

In *Rebuilding Your Broken World* by Gordon MacDonald, the author tells of Dr. Raymond Buker, who had been an Olympic athlete, and strangely enough, he had run in the 1924 Olympic Games where Eric Liddell had made his mark on athletic history.

When Buker wrote to me in some of my darkest hours, it was as if he had been reading my mind because he said:

"Dear Gordon:

Back in 1923 I once ran an invitational race (one mile) with Joey Ray and Ray Watson. We three were members of the relay team that set the world record for the four mile relay held for over twenty years. These two had a better time than I by three or four seconds. They never beat me in a race; I never did well without competition.

Anyhow in this race we three were running along at a mile rate together—the first lap, then the second lap. I suddenly hit a branch of a tree, a solid branch, [with] my left shoulder. It was a terrible blow and stopped me cold. The blow almost knocked me out. For two or three seconds I could not think. I cannot remember whether it knocked me to the ground, but it knocked me out of my running place, stopped me cold. I remember trying to figure out what I should do next. How could I ever catch them—should I bother to stay in the race.

Everyone would understand that the blow by the tree branch knocked me out. Somehow I staggered back on the track and stumbled along. I can see them (now) many, many yards ahead of me.

But I remember one clear conclusion. I must keep going—even if I come in long behind. I must not quit. So I kept going. I won the race."

This then is the lesson I learned: whatever the difficulty—the blow—we must keep on. God will lead to the result that will glorify Him.

That's Godly purpose. That's Godly perseverance. That's Godly patience.

Do you want to know about the value of perseverance in facing adversity, rejection and opposition? Check this. A page from John Wesley's diary reads as follows:

Sunday morning, May 5, preached in St. Ann's, was asked not to come back anymore.

Sunday p.m., May 5, preached at St. John's, deacons said, "Get out and stay out."

Sunday a.m., May 12, preached at St. Jude's, can't go back there either.

Sunday p.m., May 12, preached at St. George's, kicked out again.

Sunday a.m., May 19, preached at St. somebody else's, deacons called special meeting and said I couldn't return.

Sunday p.m., May 19, preached on the street, kicked off the street.

Sunday a.m., May 26, preached in meadow, chased out of meadow as a bull was turned loose during the services.

Sunday a.m., June 2, preached out at the edge of town, kicked off the highway.

Sunday p.m., June 2, afternoon service, preached in a pasture, 10,000 people came to hear me.

That's purpose. That's perseverance. That's patience.

I'm not comparing John Wesley's preaching with a Big Mac, but victory does take persistence. It took twenty-two years for the McDonald's hamburger chain to make its first billion dollars. It took IBM forty-six years and Xerox sixty-three years to make their first billion. If only we would apply that kind of determination and staying power to our walk with God. If only we could harness Wesley's ability to keep our eye on the goal and to keep on keeping on.

That's purpose. That's perseverance. That's patience.

In a sense, athletes who achieve much have learned to be content with their lot without being satisfied with your achievements. They're goal-oriented. They understand that obstacles are what you see when you take your eyes off the goal.

Sport can reflect life. In order to achieve great things you must put in the sweat, labor, and pain commensurate with your goal. The higher your goal, the more that will be required of you.

A wise man said, "Whoever among us has, through personal experience, learned what pain and suffering really are . . . belongs no more to himself alone; he is brother of all who suffer." Randy Becton knows about suffering. He has literally faced death from cancer countless times in the last twenty or more years. But each time he has been delivered from "the valley of the shadow" he has rebounded to serve the Lord in ever increasing dedication.

Paul alludes to this "brotherhood of sufferers" when he says "If we are distressed, it is for your comfort and salvation; if we are comforted, it is for your comfort, which produces in you patient endurance of the same sufferings we suffer" (2 Corinthians 1:6).

That's purpose. That's perseverance. That's patience.

To be patient is to be like the Lord: "But for that very reason I was shown mercy so that in me, the worst of sinners, Christ Jesus might display his unlimited patience as an example for those who would believe on him and receive eternal life" (1 Timothy 1:16).

The Old Testament history of the Hebrews was an endless cycle of their refusing to listen to God and their failure to remember what He had done for them—and yet He was patient and preserved them "until the fullness of time" had come. "The Lord is not slow in keeping his promise, as some understand slowness. He is patient with you, not wanting anyone to perish, but everyone to come to repentance" (2 Peter 3:9). To belong to the Lord, we must learn to partake in His patience.

And what does the patience of God have to do with "the boys of summer," bicycling, football, Vince Lombardi, Calvin Peete, or track and field? They're parables on patience. Athletes don't achieve great goals without paying the price. We won't either. And the biggest game of all is this thing we call Life. It's not like a game where some players participate while others sit on the bench. In this game, we all play. The choice for us is do we play impatiently? Or do we play with patience?

When Jesus became human almost 2000 years ago, he did not bring a summer past-time, a spectator sport, or a fleeting fantasy. He brought a kingdom with demands and a promise. In His kingdom, He said the last would be first; losers would be winners, not just for a few moments in October but for all eternity. In His kingdom, we don't celebrate vicariously through the victories of others. We have our own victory. We don't have to dream or to latch on to some other's coattails. When we lose ourselves in Him, we win, and the "cloud of witnesses" cheering us on makes ticker-tape parades seem truly temporary and trivial. October 1991 witnessed a great World Series. But it was all minor league minutiae compared to the victory we "losers" can win in Christ Jesus.

CHAPTER 7
God Is A Gentleman of Leisure

In its brief six weeks of life the worker honeybee is, well—is as busy as a bee.

It spends its first three weeks doing housekeeping chores such as cleaning and building cells in the hive, feeding larvae, tending the queen, and storing honey. In the final three weeks of its life, the worker bee forages for nectar and pollen outside the hive—flying a total of up to 1,000 miles during this period and burning up energy at a fantastic rate.

Besides its phenomenal toil, a honeybee is amazingly intelligent, or at least instinctively gifted to a high degree. A honeybee's brain weighs about one milligram. It would take 28,000 of them to equal an ounce. But a honeybee possesses complex navigational and communications skills. They use a symbolic "dance" language to convey to other bees the location of regions for nectar and pollen.

Honeybees are among the most fascinating and sophisticated of social insects, and the organization of a honeybee colony is one of the wonders of God's creation. It is a matriarchal world, headed by a queen who at the height of the breeding season may lay 2,000 eggs a day and more than a million in her life span of three to five years. Practically all of the queen's offspring are worker bees, who like herself are female. Whether a larval female grows into a queen or a worker depends on certain proteins in her food, known as royal jelly.

Each hive contains only a few males, called drones, who serve no purpose except to mate with a queen during one of her brief nuptial flights.

When it's time for a queen to mate, she leaves the hive and heads for special "drone congregation areas" which remain the same year after year. The queen begins flying higher and higher in the air, with the drones in pursuit. The drones begin falling away, from the weakest to the strongest, and the last one able to keep up with the queen will mate with her. Scientists are baffled as to how bees know where to find these congregation areas. A queen makes mating flights only during one two-week span early in her life, and there's no overlap in a hive's drone population from year to year. But somehow the bees know—generation to generation—how to congregate in the same spot.

Breeding begins soon after the winter solstice, when lengthening days cause the queen to start laying eggs. By late spring, when the colony has reached maybe 30,000 to 70,000 individuals, the queen flies off in a swarm with about half the hive's workers to start another colony. A new queen emerges to take over her mother's reproductive chores in the old hive.

When the breeding season ends, the drones are kicked out of the hive. Since drones don't have a stinger, they're defenseless, and they don't have foraging skills for survival, so they're just really kicked out to die.

Without bees to pollinate plants and trees, much of agriculture would grind to a screeching halt. Since bees are so vital to agriculture, scientists have studied them intensively and have learned some amazing things.

One bee may visit 400 flowers on a single foraging excursion outside the hive.

It requires 80,000 bee trips to produce one pound of honey.
Bees usually forage in a radius of two or three miles from their hive.

A colony subsists all winter on stored honey and may perish if the beekeeper does not leave enough honey in the hive when robbing it.

Worker bees are appropriately named. Besides cleaning and defending the hive, being nursemaids to larvae, and gathering pollen and nectar, they also maintain the hive at a constant 93 degrees Fahrenheit year-round. In hot weather the bees bring in drops of water and fan their wings to evaporate it for cooling, and in winter they cluster around the hive in layers like a blanket of warm bodies to conserve heat.

"Bees are one of the most amazing things that ever was," a beekeeper once told me. What those insects accomplish through their single-minded dedication to their task is astonishing. It's analogous to patience. They ignore, fly around, and otherwise deal with the obstacles getting in their way—but the bee keeps on keeping on, doing the job assigned to her.

That perseverance is a reflection of the nature of God, the bee's Creator. He's our Creator too, and we reflect traces of that perserverance.

The world of nature and of agriculture contains many examples of patience and its value. James urges his readers, "Be patient, then, brothers, until the Lord's coming. See how the farmer waits for the land to yield its valuable crop and how patient he is for the autumn and spring rains" (James 5:7).

Peter reinforces the requirement that we develop this thing called patience: "Through these he has given us his very great and precious promises, so that through them you may participate in the divine nature and escape the corruption in the world caused by evil desires. For this very reason, make every effort to add to your faith goodness; and to goodness, knowledge; and to knowledge, self-control; and to self-control, perseverance; and to perseverance, godliness; and to godliness, brotherly kindness; and to brotherly kindness, love" (2 Peter 1:4-7).

Without patience (or perseverance) we can't raise a crop, play a game well, or succeed in being God's child. Every champion has either developed patience—or has failed; every farmer who ever harvested a crop has waited patiently for it to ripen; every person who has known God's blessing has waited patiently to see what God wanted him or her to do.

If patience is essential in the farmer's fields, and the other ordinary affairs of life, it is more vital in the field of our spiritual maturity. If in our quest for Christ-likeness we have no patience, we're doomed to fizzle. But if we with patience persist, we are sure to gather our reward. Paul puts it this way: "Let us not become weary in doing good, for at the proper time we will reap a harvest if we do not give up" (Galatians 6:9).

We must have endurance for the waiting and testing time. It is never right to do wrong, and it's never wrong to do right. We must not be misled by the subtlety that "The end justifies the means," because this will assure our downfall. Always we must ask, "What is right?" And we must do right even if the heavens fall—or even if we must endure what we don't want to endure. The poet has said,

If thou canst plan a noble deed,
    And never flag till it succeed,
Though in the strife thy heart must bleed.
    Whatever obstacles control,
Thine hour will come, go on true soul,
    Thou'lt win the prize,
Thou'lt reach the goal.

It's a never-ending struggle. You never will arrive at perfect patience. In fact, if you feel like you've arrived you'd better reconsider. If you think you're green, you're growing; if you think you're ripe, you're rotten.

All fruitful achievements require a certain amount of time. When you plant a seed in the ground you must wait for the sun and the rain and the nourishment of the soil to do their work. Any attempt to hurry up the process will retard the growth or cause it to be poor quality. Again, you cannot change the rhythm of life, and you cannot force things beyond their natural boundaries without doing some damage.

God typically works in nature with calm leisureliness. He isn't pressured by the constraints of time. Jesus, in his earthly sojourn, naturally exhibited this same pattern. As we noted before, don't you know that the patience of Jairus was profoundly tested when Jesus was journeying to his home to heal his sick daughter. Jesus stopped along the way to help others. It must have seemed like lunacy to Jairus. But Jesus said, "Fear not, only believe."

That's what He is asking of us as we face life's ups and downs: "Fear not, only believe."

I used to have a bumper sticker on the side of my wheelchair which said, "It's Not the Ups and Downs that Bother Me—It's the *Jerks*." Our problem is that our faith isn't always strong enough to sustain us in the present—to put up with the "jerks," therefore we can't visualize the ultimate harvest. It's the old cliche about not being able to see the forest for the trees. Anyone can count the seeds in an apple, but seemingly only God is sufficiently patient to take the long view and to count the apples in a seed. The seed of our harvest is planted—if we can patiently wait to possess its bounty.

Like a farmer waiting for the harvest (assuming, of course, that we have done the necessary planting), we wait for the fruit of our labor. We don't yet possess it. In fact, we can't even see it. "But if we hope for what we do not yet have, we wait for it patiently" (Romans 8:25).

Hesiod, Greek poet of the eighth century B.C., observed that

> Badness you can get easily, in quantity: the road is smooth, and it lies close by. But in front of excellence the immortal gods have put sweat, and long and steep is the way to it, and rough at first. But when you come to the top, then it is easy, even though it is hard.

That describes the road to patience. To paraphrase Hesiod, you might say that "Impatience you can get easily, in quantity: the road is smooth, and it lies close by. But in front of *patience* the immortal gods have put sweat, and long and steep is the way to it, and rough at first. But when you come to the top, then it is easy, even though it is hard." Patience is a natural outgrowth of Christian maturity. As Paul told the Christians in Galatia, " . . . the fruit of the Spirit is love, joy, peace, patience, kindness, goodness, faithfulness, gentleness and self-control. Against such things there is no law" (Galatians 5:22, 23).

We aspire to such heights, and that's commendable. And we need to be patient with ourselves as well as with others. But we should be *attaining* a higher plateau now and then— and not merely always trying. Those who live in the mountains have a longer day than those who live in the valley. Sometimes all we need to brighten our day is to rise a little higher. To understand is one thing; to do is another. Thinking well is wise, planning well is wiser, but doing well is wisest.

It happened in Southwest Asia in the 14th century. The army of the conqueror Emperor Tamerlane (a descendant of Ghengis Khan) had been thrashed, scattered by a powerful enemy. Tamerlane himself was hiding in a deserted stable while enemy troops combed the countryside looking for him.

As he lay there, desperate and defeated, Tamerlane watched an ant try to carry a grain of corn over a perpendicular wall. The kernel was larger than the ant itself. The emperor counted the attempts—sixty-nine times the ant tried to carry it up the wall. Sixty-nine times it fell back. On the seventieth effort the ant pushed the grain of corn over the top.

Tamerlane jumped to his feet with a shout. He could see that he, too, would prevail in the end. And he did, reorganizing his army and putting the enemy to flight. Big lessons sometimes come from small teachers.

A few weeks ago my Dad planted some marigold seeds. They were shriveled and ugly. He put them in the dark soil and watered them, and something happened to those seeds. The husks cracked. They started to sprout little green shoots. The water, the soil, the sunshine—and the miracle of growth. Those little plants came up the ugliest, scrawniest seedlings you've ever seen. Down at the end of the row Dad drove a stake in the ground, and on that stake he tacked the empty seed packet with a picture of beautiful marigolds on it. Some gardeners do this so they can remember what they planted where. Dad said, "I did it so those little ugly seedlings could see their potential—their destiny. Right now the plants are frail and ungainly. I want them to see that picture at the end of the row and say, 'Hey, that's beautiful. That's what we are meant to be—and with God's help, we will be.'"

Every evil habit and attitude—including impatience—must come before God's scrutiny. That's not especially easy for any of us—especially when the aroma of our spiritual arrogance has numbed the yearning for patience. Too often, I can identify with Dorothy, the Cowardly Lion, the Tin Man, and the Scarecrow in the Wizard of Oz. They nearly succumbed to the aromatic spell of the poppies—even though Oz was within their sight. We must cast off any spiritual drowsiness and move on toward Godly goals.

Every morning you are handed twenty-four brand-new hours. They're one of the few things in the world you get free of charge. Your health may cost money to achieve or regain, but these twenty-four hours cost you absolutely nothing. If you were as rich as Rockefeller, you couldn't buy even one extra hour. If you were the lowest scoundrel on the planet, you couldn't be deprived of a single minute. So in this respect we are all truly "created equal"—from the richest to the poorest.

What do you do with this priceless treasure? How do you invest it? Remember, you have to use it as given at once. You can't save up a few years for your old age. And if you mess it up, you can't ask for a refund. If you lose it, then it's just gone. There is no "lost and found" window. Every minute, every hour, and every second must be put to use immediately.

You can see that wasted time is an even greater misfortune than wasted money or wasted health. You might regain those things if you lost them, but hours, days, months, and years wasted are gone forever. Confucius is quoted as saying, "The nature of man never changes; it is only his habits that separate men." Patience is a habit that will help make your minutes count for eternity.

A little girl came bouncing into the kitchen one morning, alive and cheery as only a child can be. Her mother, with only one eye awake, was dragging gloomily through the motions of making breakfast.

"Mommy, aren't you happy today?" asked the little girl.

"Sure, I'm happy," her mother assured her without much enthusiasm.

"Well," answered the child, "you sure haven't told your face about it yet." It's a common problem. If we are happy with life, we sure fail to show it on our faces—or in our actions. And this means that our minds and hearts don't know much about it either. We hunger for satisfaction. We pursue it. We long for it. "But we ask and do not receive." We want *now* what actually must first be planted, cultivated, and eventually harvested. But that's the end result. It doesn't become ours until later.

> Life itself can't give us joy
>   Unless we really will it.
> Life just gives us the time and place—
>   It's up to us to fill it.
>
> —author unknown

The question is what do we fill it with? What builds a satisfying and satisfied life? With nature as a model, here's the secret to a gratifying life now and an eternal life later: plant the best seeds and wait for the harvest. There are three essentials. First, *you need a self you can live with*. You may have a lot of things, or you may lack most of this world's treasures and trinkets. We need some of those things to feed, house, and clothe us. But nobody will ever find complete satisfaction in placing money as the goal for living. Those holding that attitude never possess enough and are always impatient for more.

John Muir, the naturalist, once commented on a wealthy tycoon who was fabulously rich, but nevertheless was compelled to devote his life to acquiring more and more money. The man was oblivious to the good things he could have done in life with his riches. "I am richer than he," Muir observed. "I have all the money I want, and he hasn't."

When William Allen White, the noted newspaper editor, decided to donate Peter Pan Park to the citizens of his hometown, Emporia, Kansas, he said, "I have always felt that there were three kicks in every dollar: one when you make it—and how I do love to make a dollar; one when you have it—and I have the Yankee lust for saving; and the third, when you give it away. The last kick is the biggest of all."

The giver always receives. The giving heart is a satisfied heart. The more he gives, the more that returns—not the least of which includes joy and fulfillment. "Give, and it will be given to you. A good measure, pressed down, shaken together and running over, will be poured into your lap. For with the measure you use, it will be measured to you" (Luke 6:38).

No doubt the Lord was familiar with the Dead Sea. It receives fresh water daily, but it holds on to all it receives. It gives out nothing in return. We can behave in that way. Or we can act like a flowing river that waters and nurtures the land through which it passes. Whether we joyfully invest ourselves in the enrichment of life around us depends on the soundness of the values we are sowing.

The meaning and satisfaction of life depends less on what we accumulate materially and more on what we share—thankful that we are privileged to do so. This isn't just a sweet idea. It's not merely a tidy thought for the day. It's a dynamic, life-shaping principle. "In everything I did, I showed you that by this kind of hard work we must help the weak, remembering the words the Lord Jesus himself said: 'It is more blessed to give than to receive'" (Acts 20:35).

This truth rings as true in the sphere of the emotional and spiritual as it does in the realm of the material.

No matter what your circumstance in life, build bridges away from yourself—bridges of interest in others, of kindness, of sharing, of trust, of patience—and you'll find that others will bring blessings to your life over the bridges you've constructed. Your own life will be warmer and richer in friends, enjoyment, usefulness, in opportunities to share and grow—and especially in an inner well-being. "The real way to happiness," said Lord Baden-Powell, founder of the Boy Scouts, "is by giving your happiness to other people. Try to leave the world a little better than you found it."

Satisfaction in living also hinges on being conscious of what to do without. We tend to burden ourselves down with senseless encumbrances and insignificant preoccupations that muddle our days and drain away our energies. Lugging these loads, we are impaired, because we can't pour our heart, mind, and energy into useful and satisfying pursuits. As Henry David Thoreau urged from Walden Pond, "Simplify, simplify!"

Experienced travelers know the value in "traveling light." They are as deliberate in what they leave out as in what they pack to take. We could benefit from similar wisdom as we pack for our journey through life. Life is challenging enough without the excess of heavy baggage such as anxiety, anger, guilt, or impatience.

A second essential for a life of patience is *a purpose to live for*. The great mass of humankind has found no satisfactory goal for which to reach, no meaning powerful enough to drive their life in any direction. The normal frustrations of living are enough to strain our patience, and catastrophic life experiences may stress us to what seems to be the breaking point. Our times are full of turmoil, exacerbated by random violence and senseless destruction, contempt for authority, a reckless indifference for human life, dashing through our days at a feverish pitch, worsened by abuse of alcohol and drugs, broken homes, and spiritual and emotional desperation. All of those things point to a people who have failed to recognize an overriding, life-directing purpose for being here. There is no unity of being for so many people. The reason for living has escaped many of us. Life is, for too many persons, "full of sound and fury, signifying nothing."

A sense of direction and purpose can exert an amazing calming influence on us. It points us toward commitment and self-discipline. Dr. John A. Logan, Jr., noted educator has said,

> . . . Paradoxical as it may seem, true freedom comes from commitment—commitment to people, to ideas, to causes, greater than oneself . . . . We are happiest when we are fully used, and it is the boredom and frustration of disengagement that makes us querulous and petty and mean . . . .

Scripture said the same thing a long time ago. Peter tells us that " . . . a man is a slave to whatever has mastered him" (2 Peter 2:19). And Paul said, "Don't you know that when you offer yourselves to someone to obey him as slaves, you are slaves to the one whom you obey—whether you are slaves to sin, which leads to death, or to obedience, which leads to righteousness?" (Romans 6:16).

The trail out of this jungle is clear. Self-discipline and commitment lead to purpose, and purpose leads to fulfillment, and fulfillment yields the patience that comes from happiness. Again, Scripture said it: " . . . but we also rejoice in our sufferings, because we know that suffering produces perseverance; perseverance, character; and character, hope" (Romans 5:3, 4).

The fact of the matter is that God created us to live for more than *self*, and impatience is a manifestation of self-centeredness. We are most unhappy when we focus on making ourselves the center of our attention, because the Father created us to serve, to achieve, and to create with others in mind. A hammer and nails lay inertly in a toolbox. They aren't fully a hammer and nails until they fulfill their destiny, the hammer pounding the nails into wood in order to build a structure. Then they are forming something new and useful. Only then are they following the plan for which they were fashioned in the first place.

It's the same with us. We are happiest when we are helping, working, sharing, serving—when we are fulfilling the design for which we were created. The real source of personal fulfillment isn't in doing great deeds. Rather, it is in the day to day living of ordinary life—preparing a meal, earning this week's paycheck, fixing a dripping faucet, tying a child's shoe, writing a note to a sick or lonely person, buying a silly "thinking of you" gift, doing the laundry, mowing the yard, sweeping the garage, overlooking sharp words. It might be in the way you greet a customer, or in taking care of a sick baby, keeping the house pretty and clean, or in doing a kindness for some older person. You may fulfill your purpose by reaching out a hand of encouragement to someone who needs it, or by bearing your heartaches with faith and persistence, or by hammering away at your misfortunes until you forge them into a blessing—to yourself and to others (many of whom you'll never even realize that you've blessed with your perseverance). We fulfill the purpose of living when we faithfully perform the mundane, ordinary, unpretentious, enduring things that life asks of us day in and day out, and we do them well, with cheer and patience.

A third essential for a life of patience is an *abiding faith*. We need something to live for and to live by. Arthur Gossip, a famous Scottish preacher of years past, had a sermon called "When Life Tumbles In." He composed it after the unexpected death of his wife. Her sudden demise was the end of the world for this man. In an instant, his life partner was gone and he was desolate. "When life tumbles in, what then?" he asked.

You can know with a certainty that it will tumble in, for each of us. The manifestations will vary, the degrees will vary, but life will for all of us come tumbling in. "Never morning wore to evening but some heart did break," said Arthur Gossip.

What do we do then, if we have no faith to live by, no spiritual underpinnings to hold us up? It's a certainty that nothing trivial will answer.

In my own experience, I've seen people who were in and out of hospitals and rehabilitation with me. Some had no faith, and they collapsed under life's burden; others had a faith, and it allowed them to achieve varying levels of acceptance and achievement; but others had the Faith, which empowered them to see their tragedy transformed into blessing.

Anyone with "a faith" is better off than someone without a faith. With enough faith in "the human spirit," you can make the best of a bad situation and salvage an acceptable life even in the worst of conditions.

But that's not the same thing as the triumph which God promises to His children: " . . . we know that in all things God works for the good of those who love him, who have been called according to his purpose" (Romans 8:28), Paul writes to assure us. That's not the same thing as "making the best of a bad situation." It's the difference between accommodation and triumph. A bedrock trust in your ultimate worth, care, and future steadies your "earthly tabernacle" while the winds of life howl at the door. I'm commending to you a hammered out certainty, formed on the anvil of life. "Now faith is being sure of what we hope for and certain of what we do not see" (Hebrews 11:1).

This kind of fundamental foundation is essential in times of crisis, but it is also a precious asset in sustaining us for the long haul of "normal" life. We need faith daily—to face this day, this week, this month, this year. And to keep on doing that.

A self you can live with, a purpose to live for, and a faith to live by, these are key essentials to a blessed life. They take time to cultivate—a lifetime, as a matter of fact. And that's what God allows us. "Bear in mind that our Lord's patience means salvation, just as our dear brother Paul also wrote you with the wisdom that God gave him" (2 Peter 3:15).

It pays to be patient. Remember the honey bee, the ant, and the farmer. "To those who by persistence in doing good seek glory, honor and immortality, he will give eternal life" (Romans 2:7). "Let us not become weary in doing good, for at the proper time we will reap a harvest if we do not give up" (Galatians 6:9).

CHAPTER 8
Are We Having Fun Yet?

"The Greeks have a word for it." In this case, there are at least two biblical Greek words to express variations in our English word "patience."

The word translated "patience" in the text of Galatians 5:22-23 is *makrothumia*, an " . . . endurance, constancy, steadfastness, perseverance; especially as shown in bearing troubles and ills." This is the idea of enduring trials, it's an attitude of mind and heart with regard to "things."

The other Greek word for patience, *hupomone*, deals with the attitude of "longsuffering" needed for dealing with people.

A mother and her four-year-old daughter are making cookies. The child is trying to use the electric hand mixer and, understandably, is having some problems. The beaters on the mixer (a thing) keep bouncing out of the mixing bowl and hurling flour, chocolate chips, and other things around the kitchen. The child is needing patience (endurance) with the thing, the mixer. At the same time, the child is not handling the mixer very well, and she's making a mess, so the mother is patient—longsuffering—with her daughter (a person).

God prizes highly the virtue of patience which, it seems, is best developed through trials. Now isn't that an unsettling thought. But it's true. Patience is a quality that develops and matures in stress, anxiety, and struggles. Read the first chapter of the book of James.

"Consider it pure joy, my brothers, whenever you face trials of many kinds, because you know that the testing of your faith develops perseverance. Perseverance must finish its work so that you may be mature and complete, not lacking anything" (James 1:2-4).

Be joyful in trials? Personally, I'd rather take the scenic route. However, the truth remains: enduring trials is what matures us into what we're capable of being. Once we're mature, we can be joyful even while struggling in our trials. That idea can be tough to understand—and that task is definitely tough to do.

"Patience is bitter, but its fruit is sweet," noted Rousseau.

A Chinese proverb notes that "Patience is power. With time and patience the lowly mulberry leaf becomes priceless silk."

There are sources of patience, and degrees of patience. If you and I are to practice patience in suffering, we've got to know exactly what it is that we are to do.

There are two types of people with patience. One is the "Naturally Patient Person," who just seems to be endowed with a calm, levelheaded mentality. The other is the "Person with Acquired Patience," who became patient through training. In either case, there are degrees of patience. Any of us can be patient as long as the provocation doesn't touch our points of sensitivity. So don't pat yourself on the back too soon. We are all cool, calm, and collected until . . . .

Several years ago, Reuel Lemmons, the late gospel preacher, was on a trip to the Holy Lands with a large group. He was a gifted speaker and a man knowledgeable in many fields. He could speak off-the-cuff, and capably, on nearly any subject. The itinerary for the day called for a flight from Jerusalem to Nicosia, Cyprus, and then to Beirut.

It was a Sunday. Before flying out, the group was to worship together on the Mount of Olives and Reuel Lemmons was to preach during the service. Lemmons' wife had severe arthritis and didn't travel much, so this trip was special to them. He was very protective of her well-being. Somehow they got assigned to separate planes for the trip to Lebanon. He began asking to be transferred to her plane so he could care for her. Then he began to insist. Departure time was nearing and his nerves were wearing thin. The airline personnel were uncooperative at best, the tour guide was no help, and in the end everyone was coolly indifferent to Lemmons' requests. By the time they arrived at the Mount of Olives for the devotional service, he was so distraught over the situation that he couldn't preach. "I'm so angry!" he said. "I'm too angry. I can't preach . . . get somebody else to do it."

Some people in the group thought his behavior was ridiculous and unbecoming to a man of his stature. But the fact was that the "trial" had touched him where he was vulnerable.

My dad was on that trip. When they arrived in Beirut, their hotel was a quaint, older facility right on the shore of the Mediterranean. It was one of those places like you see in the movies. Someone complained to the tour guide about the "old hotel" they were in. It wasn't a four-star facility, but it was nice and the ambiance was superb. The next thing everyone knew there was a "knock, knock" on the door and the tour guide announcing, "Pack your things, we are moving in thirty minutes."

And they moved—to downtown Beirut, with a view of other modern skyscraper hotels. This forced relocation irritated a lot of people in the tour group—some of the same folks who had thought Reuel Lemmons' earlier aggravation was a shame. But now it was their panic button that was getting pushed. It all depends, doesn't it? When it's someone else's impatience that's showing, we can smugly say "I'd never act like that." Ah, but the worm turns . . . and when a provocation hits home, our patience is often short fused.

But patience is good for us. I heard about two men who were diagnosed as having tuberculosis. The year was 1927. Medical science had little to offer them. One man went home angry. He ranted and raved, denying the reality of what faced him. The second man was concerned over the seriousness of his condition, of course. He knew that he couldn't work, and that he'd need to isolate himself. "I've gotten behind in my reading," he said. "Now I'll catch up." He devoted himself to reading, to study, and to prayer. In fact, he reinvigorated his faith and turned himself over to the Lord. He was a relaxed and peaceful man. Six months later, his tuberculosis was in remission and he showed no signs of disease. In his case, patience was actually healing.

Many times, if instead of working ourselves into a stressed out condition we'd just put our hand in the Lord's hand, then "in patience we are healed."

God has designed a sacred solution to the problem of human suffering. Maybe you can be cool, calm, and collected while somebody else undergoes a trial. Most of us can manage that trick too. But what if it's your trial? Is that a different story? It's not enough to "be cool until I'm not." We've got to mature to the point of patience—even in the middle of our own severe trials.

We all react so differently. I remember Miss Bertha Linn, a fine lady in her nineties. Her "baby brother" had just died, in his eighties. She was the last survivor in her family and was now alone in the world except for nieces and nephews. Her health was frail, she was living in a nursing home, and she couldn't attend her brother's funeral. Her niece sat with her during the time of the service for Howard. Miss Bertha's mind was as sharp as the proverbial tack. "I wonder why God let's me lay here like this?" she asked. "I'm old, worn out, and useless, and Howard was still active and useful—but he died. I wonder if the Lord has forgotten that I'm still here?"

But I know why Miss Bertha was still alive. Even in the nursing home, she never stopped keeping up with who had new babies at church, she never quit sending her weekly contribution, and she knew all about the latest congregational activities. That's what she talked about with her visitors, which she had plenty of. Young mothers even brought little children to see Miss Bertha—ever the first grade teacher—and she'd sing Bible songs with them there in her nursing home room. Miss Bertha was still among the living because she was showing a lot of people how to grow old, and how to endure trials gracefully as a Christian.

I knew of an aging man, in his late seventies. His wife had died, and his health wasn't good—though there was nothing life threatening. He withdrew from life, shutting himself away from everybody. When neighbors didn't see any activity at his house for several days, they called the police, who found that the man had shot himself. He couldn't handle life. I don't understand why we are made like we are. I don't fully understand why some people, such as Miss Bertha, can tolerate life's stresses, while others can't.

Look again at what James says to us:

James, a servant of God and of the Lord Jesus Christ, To the twelve tribes scattered among the nations: Greetings. Consider it pure joy, my brothers, whenever you face trials of many kinds, because you know that the testing of your faith develops perseverance. Perseverance must finish its work so that you may be mature and complete, not lacking anything (James 1:1-4).

If you're a *Star Trek* fan, you know about the "Prime Directive" of the United Federation of Planets. Well, James is giving Christians a prime directive. We are at war. Life is a warfare. We're at war with Satan, with his followers, with things—but James says "consider it pure joy" when you face battles. You've got to have patience, endurance, and longsuffering in these trials—no matter where they originate. We're all going to be tested, every one of us. Job said it, "'Man born of woman is of few days and full of trouble'" (Job 14:1).

You won't go into God's glory without testing. You are going to be given the opportunity to undergo trials of some description. You will be offered the opportunity of saying, "I have fought the good fight, I have kept the faith, I have finished the course" under the circumstances that came into my life.

Sometimes the need for patient acceptance is terribly painful. When someone has with malice done you a great harm, it is time for patience. When, in the name of having a good time, some drunken driver injures or kills a loved one, it's time to call on patience. When a vile man chooses to rape the innocent, it's time to call on patience. At these times, patience is all that can carry us through to acceptance and forgiveness. It isn't easy, and the price is costly. But real forgiveness is always costly. Just look at the cross. That's where the price was actually paid. We can be patient.

James 1:3 is your *"Stress Preparedness Kit,"* "because you know that the testing of your faith develops perseverance." James assumes the inevitability of testing and trials. You will have them. Just know that you will be tested, you will be tried, you will be stressed, you will be anxious, you will endure catastrophes, you will suffer. So get ready for it with your head held high and with thanksgiving in your heart. A Christian is a child of the King, and those who abide in the Lord can triumph where others can't. Children of the King are distinctive, special, different.

If you're not different, you have problems ahead of you. If you're not different, then you've got to get on that road today, to become different—with the Lord's help.

I think James is telling us to use the little annoyances of daily life as exercise to strengthen ourselves against the larger calamities which will come. That's why he says to "consider it pure joy" when we meet trials—and it makes sense. If we view them as preparation and training for our own good, we can be joyful even though tried and stressed. If we learn to bear everyday trials and distresses quietly and calmly, then when the big storms roll ashore our strength won't fail us.

Plan ahead. Prepare. Build yourself up for stresses and griefs that are yet to come your way. It can be done. "Do not be anxious about anything, but in everything, by prayer and petition, with thanksgiving, present your requests to God. And the peace of God, which transcends all understanding, will guard your hearts and your minds in Christ Jesus" (Philippians 4:6,7).

Put your hand in the Savior's hand and He will see you through—even through "the valley of the shadow."

In January and February of 1992, the Fort Worth *Star-Telegram* carried two op-ed type of letters from readers. They contrast the two basic kinds of responses to life's challenges. The second letter, a response to an earlier one, was titled "Sorrow Over Lack of Belief." The letter was from Melanie Merth. It said,

This is in response to Joe Rooney's Jan. 9 letter about no faith in God. As I write this, I feel no anger over his feelings about Christians clinging to "fantasy," or that we should just live for ourselves today, or that we are born alone and we will die alone. I feel deep sorrow for him. Maybe Rooney has had a series of hurtful situations, or feels that if there is a God where is He? Maybe he feels the way we Christians sometimes feel—if we're willing to admit it—that if God is in control, why is this world in the shape that it's in? We all have questions, Christians and non- Christians alike, about this matter. The part that worries me is that Rooney has no hope, just the day to day grind of living. There's more to life than that. If I could spend a couple of hours with him I could tell him how my life has been for the last four years and he would ask me, "Why haven't you lost your mind?" It's been more than rough. All I can say is I wasn't born alone—God planned it. I won't die alone—Jesus will be there. I'm never alone—the Holy Spirit is always with me. Maybe Rooney has been around so-called Christians, ones who talk that they're Christians, but live a life of hypocrisy. Maybe that's the problem. There are many of them. However, there are many more Christians who acknowledge that Christ is God's son, and that though the life we lead may be rough we cling to the cross during good times and during bad times. My sorrow is for the hardness of Rooney's heart. How I wish he knew how God, Jesus, and the Holy Spirit long for him, and love him and all others who feel the way he does.

"There are times," says Wyatt Sawyer, a gospel preacher, "when all that God asks of us is silence, tears, and patience. Most of us have wept; all of us will."

In those moments, you've got to have patience or you're lost. Listen again to what James advises:

If any of you lacks wisdom, he should ask God, who gives generously to all without finding fault, and it will be given to him. But when he asks, he must believe and not doubt, because he who doubts is like a wave of the sea, blown and tossed by the wind. That man should not think he will receive anything from the Lord; he is a double-minded man, unstable in all he does (James 1:5-8).

Prayer is a source for God-given patience and wisdom—and the two things are not far apart. You've got to believe, and you've got to ask.

When you're inundated in one of life's grotesque experiences—such as my crippling polio, or the too soon death of my younger sister at age 30 with cancer—sometimes, when you're in the response stage of anger, not prayer, not God, not Jesus, not the Holy Spirit, not the Scripture, not poetry, not friends—nothing reaches through the anger for a time. That's normal, at the first. When the horror and hurt are deep enough, nothing relieves it in the beginning. It takes time. You have to pray for strength and wisdom and patience, and you have to grow in the Spirit. You never let go of the Hand. But for a time—and it's okay to say it—nothing helps the hurt. You don't heal if you don't hurt.

And in time, God, Jesus, the Spirit, the Scripture, friends, love, poetry, flowers eventually reach you when you're ready. So even in the deepest agonies, expect the healing, watch for it, desire it.

The comfort is there. In 2 Corinthians 1:2-7, Paul says,

> Grace and peace to you from God our Father and the Lord Jesus Christ. Praise be to the God and Father of our Lord Jesus Christ, the Father of compassion and the God of all comfort, who comforts us in all our troubles, so that we can comfort those in any trouble with the comfort we ourselves have received from God. For just as the sufferings of Christ flow over into our lives, so also through Christ our comfort overflows. If we are distressed, it is for your comfort and salvation; if we are comforted, it is for your comfort, which produces in you patient endurance of the same sufferings we suffer. And our hope for you is firm, because we know that just as you share in our sufferings, so also you share in our comfort.

When you are severely tried, and the stress is building up,

read that passage. It calms the storm. It reminds us of hope. It tells you that comfort comes from above, "from God our Father and the Lord Jesus Christ." When you're ready for comfort, it comes from above.

In James 5:7-11 you can read about examples of patience in people under intense apprehension.

> Be patient, then, brothers, until the Lord's coming. See how the farmer waits for the land to yield its valuable crop and how patient he is for the autumn and spring rains. You too, be patient and stand firm, because the Lord's coming is near. Don't grumble against each other, brothers, or you will be judged. The Judge is standing at the door! Brothers, as an example of patience in the face of suffering, take the prophets who spoke in the name of the Lord. As you know, we consider blessed those who have persevered. You have heard of Job's perseverance and have seen what the Lord finally brought about. The Lord is full of compassion and mercy.

That last verse is our faith—the Lord is compassionate and merciful.

Think about the farmer. Think about the prophets, and Job. Think about Abraham. Think about Moses. Think about Paul—imprisoned, beaten, shipwrecked. Think about Stephen. Most of all, think about Jesus on the cross. They made it. They persevered. And if they can, we can.

Patience is the courage of the warrior. Paul tells us that we are more than conquerors through Him that loved us. Patience is our strength against fate.

Everything comes to the person who will only wait. Someone has said, "He who can have patience can have what he wills."

Patience is the power of God's Spirit, working through us, to triumph over circumstance.

CHAPTER 9

Your Goat Will Get Got

When it comes to our battle with impatience, the words of the old comic strip character Pogo ring true: "We has met the enemy, and he is us."

Writing in the fourth century, the historian Eusebius relates the terrible persecutions and torture that the Roman emperors inflicted on Christians. They were fed to voracious lions and dogs, they were grilled alive on red-hot grates, and they were lashed with cat-o'-nine-tails tipped with jagged pieces of metal or bone. Sometimes they were scourged until they were actually disemboweled.

They didn't have to endure all of this. These horrible agonies could have been escaped if those Christians had only mouthed the words "Caesar is lord." They didn't even need to believe it—just say the words. And yet thousands chose agonizing death rather than the simple, expedient, painless way out of this. Why did they do that? And *how* did they do that? How could they willingly endure so much?

In his book *Unlimited Power*, Anthony Robbins comments on what he calls the Power of Pain. "There are only two reasons why people do things," he says. "To gain pleasure, or to avoid pain."

Since those early Christians associated martyrdom with the promise of reaching heaven (our ultimate "pleasure"), and they associated renouncing Jesus as Lord with the ultimate pain of eternal exile in Hell, then they were empowered to patiently endure excruciating pain. By linking certain concepts, they were able—with God's help—to accept the unacceptable. We can do that same thing. Thank God that we probably won't be called upon to endure the hideous torture for our faith that the early believers faced. But we do face our personal stresses and strains of life which can tax our patience and burden our relationships. Sometime, somewhere, somebody or something will "get your goat." It's not "if," but "when." Your spouse is "always" late. Your boss is forever pressuring, pushing, and rushing you. The kids "never" do what you tell them to do. Somebody who is important to you is consistently thoughtless of your feelings. A jar lid refuses to open. A nail bends under the blows of your hammer. A golf ball hooks into the rough instead of going straight on the green. These and ten thousand other instances can trigger our impatience, our anger. There are big and little frustrations that try us. The impatient life is like a hammer without a head, because the impatient person is always flying off the handle. It happens so easily, especially if the provocation touches us where it hurts most. There are annoyances in the home, or at work, or even while driving down the highway, that can cause our patience to slip—or even to crash and burn. There's no shortage of provocations.

I seem to fit in that category of people mentioned in the previous chapter—those who are "naturally" patient. Or maybe that should be "patient by nature." But that doesn't mean that I—or others with a calm disposition—never feel impatience. It's only our mode of reaction that differs. Where some scream, hit, and throw things, others tend to get quiet, to seethe. I assure you that in using my left foot to learn to paint in oils, to use a computer, to use a telephone, read a book, to hold a newspaper, to send Morse code on Ham radio, to sign my name with my toes—those and other skills were not developed without banging into severe frustration. And it's not over yet. I still encounter obstacles—daily, by the hour, by the minute.

If I drop something on the floor, I can't pick it up. It's annoying enough to have to ask someone else to do it for me, and sometimes when I'm home alone and drop something it is going to stay on the floor awhile. No matter if it's an important floppy disk from the computer that can be ruined if I run all over it with my wheelchair. It's on the floor until someone shows up to pick it up.

Frustration also hits me at times because I can't come and go on my own schedule. Besides the obvious hindrance of not driving, I'm also limited by the amount of time I can be away from my respirator. Polio fouled up the nerves controlling my diaphragm, the muscle which makes us breathe. My breathing is a conscious effort, using muscles in my neck and chest. After two or three hours of breathing on my own (two or three times daily), I must get back to my positive pressure machine. I hold the hose in my hand (it is good for this job) and I take air by holding a mouthpiece in my lips. It's no big deal, I can do other things while "breathing." But I can't go farther than this four-foot hose. All of which means that I must pick and choose where I want to invest my time away from the respirator. And that can be frustrating. But all of us have these kinds of choices to some degree—not just those of us using respirators.

Which brings us back where we started. If there are provocations to the right of us, and provocations to the left of us—like the cannons in *The Charge of the Light Brigade*—how can we ever learn to react with patience?

You begin by changing the *automatic sequence of events*. Get a pencil and paper—do it now—and write down five reasons why you must get rid of your impatience. You might write, "If I don't learn to control my impatience, I'll create problems of resentment between myself and my spouse." Or "I must be more patient with the kids or they'll start kicking the dog and the dog will bite the postman and he will sue me and we will be evicted from our home in order to sell it to satisfy the postman's suit against us."

Or you might well include "I need to be more patient so that I can be more like my Heavenly Father, who is infinitely patient with me."

Be honest with yourself in making your list. List the top five reasons why *YOU* need to be more patient. Meditate on this, pray about it. Envision the worst consequences of your impatience and anger—where will they lead?

Jot down a list of how and what you feel inside when impatience rears its ugly head. There are physical manifestations: your heart rate increases, your breathing quickens, you feel hot, you may blush red in the face.

Now make a list of five *beneficial* things that will occur when you are patient. "If I'm more patient with the children, they will have a better self-image and will grow up to be successful and wealthy people who will take good care of me in my old age." Again, be specific. Be realistic about your own situation.

Now you have new motivations—new goals to envision—for helping you to be more patient.

The only problem is that you're still the same old you. The aggravations that trigger your impatience are still there. Now you need to interrupt that *automatic sequence of events* which leads to impatient reactions. When something or someone gets your goat, when an exposed nerve gets punched, and you start to lose your cool—do something unexpected, concrete, and really off the wall. Say, "No Billy Goat Gruff today." Or "That's your tax dollars at work." Or—as the old adage says—bite your tongue. Really. Do anything that will interrupt your usual *automatic sequence of events.* This will give your rational mind a chance to change your course.

Now remind yourself how you should act in the present situation—and then require of yourself that you act in that way, right now. Each victory will empower you for future victories. You will, in time, change the way you react to stressful provocations. You will create within yourself, with God's help, a new mindset by "the renewing of your mind."

It won't happen "in one easy lesson." But if you keep on keeping on with the effort, you will eventually replace your impatient response patterns with responses that are patient. In effect, you will keep reminding yourself of the bad consequences (pain) of your impatience, which you'll want to avoid; and you will remind yourself of the good that results (pleasure) from your patience, which you'll want to seek. The old unpleasurable ways will be supplanted by new beneficial ways of behaving.

You can make these things happen just by thinking about them. "Create in me a pure heart, O God, and renew a steadfast spirit within me" (Psalm 51:10). "The sacrifices of God are a broken spirit; a broken and contrite heart, O God, you will not despise" (Psalm 51:17). "Teach us to number our days aright, that we may gain a heart of wisdom" (Psalm 90:12). "His heart is secure, he will have no fear; in the end he will look in triumph on his foes" (Psalm 112:8). "I have hidden your word in my heart that I might not sin against you" (Psalm 119:11). "I have chosen the way of truth; I have set my heart on your laws" (Psalm 119:30). "I run in the path of your commands, for you have set my heart free" (Psalm 119:32). "I have sought your face with all my heart; be gracious to me according to your promise" (Psalm 119:58). "Search me, O God, and know my heart; test me and know my anxious thoughts" (Psalm 139:23).

Know what you want to achieve. Look at your list of five beneficial things that will occur when you are patient. Maybe your list began with more than five items. If so, do some weeding. Mark out the less vital entries. Condense the list to only those goals which are most insistent. As the list shrinks to five items, you'll discover that the remaining goals have increasing necessity for you.

Keep the intensity of your desire for patience burning bright. Keep visualizing—in specific detail—the benefits (pleasure) of achieving a fuller measure of patience. And understand that by asking God to increase your patience, and by seeking to build your ability to react patiently, you may very well be presented with new and unexpected opportunities for displaying patience. I know a lady who prayed for patience. "And the Lord answered by sending me twins," she says. The results you achieve may well exceed anything you could have dreamed or imagined.

Believe that what you seek will happen. "If you believe, you will receive whatever you ask for in prayer" (Matthew 21:22). Write this verse, and your five reasons for seeking patience on a file card and carry it with you. Use some system for reviewing it several times daily—maybe after each meal, or every time you use the telephone. But somehow manage to stop what you're doing and then read (aloud if possible) your patience goals and the Lord's affirmation that you will reach them.

Be thankful. Thankfulness is an energizing, cleansing emotion. "Do not be anxious about anything, but in everything, by prayer and petition, with thanksgiving, present your requests to God." What happens then? "And the peace of God, which transcends all understanding, will guard your hearts and your minds in Christ Jesus" (Philippians 4:6,7). Gratitude sweeps away the poison of impatience, fear, and anger. Feel gratitude for each opportunity to learn patience. The events themselves may not be pleasant, but we can be grateful for the chance to grow and mature in the likeness of Christ.

Trust in the outcome. Remember that trust is the link between the world of faith and the realization of that faith. "And we know that in all things God works for the good of those who love him, who have been called according to his purpose" (Romans 8:28). You must trust in the One who gives that assurance, then you must invite His testing and training, and then you must allow His ways and His patience to fill your life.

Our big problem with having patience is our impatience. Really. We want patience, but we're impatient about undergoing the training to get it. You see, the aggravations that produce genuine patience are worse than fingernails on a chalkboard. Serious illness can test your mettle. A lifelong disability can strain your resolve to seek patience. A permanent "thorn in the flesh" of any kind can become tiresome after a while, especially when you've prayed to the Lord again and again to remove it—and His answer keeps coming back "My grace is enough for you."

Our attitude is "I don't mind being tested, but how long will this last? I've got plans for Thursday." What happens when the situation is here to stay?

"Be patient, then, brothers, until the Lord's coming" (James 5:7). That's God's will, and His strong admonition to us.

> In this you greatly rejoice, though now for a little while you may have had to suffer grief in all kinds of trials. These have come so that your faith—of greater worth than gold, which perishes even though refined by fire—may be proved genuine and may result in praise, glory and honor when Jesus Christ is

revealed. Though you have not seen him, you love him; and even though you do not see him now, you believe in him and are filled with an inexpressible and glorious joy, for you are receiving the goal of your faith, the salvation of your souls (1 Peter 1:6-9).

How can trials be "an inexpressible and glorious joy"? "Because you know that the testing of your faith develops perseverance. Perseverance must finish its work so that you may be mature and complete, not lacking anything" (James 1:3,4).

Notice what we get—"*mature and complete, not lacking anything.*" Each day renews our struggle for perfection so that we may not lack anything. The abundant life includes patience. "We proclaim him, admonishing and teaching everyone with all wisdom, so that we may present everyone perfect in Christ" (Colossians 1:28). That's why "You need to persevere so that when you have done the will of God, you will receive what he has promised" (Hebrews 10:36).

What promise? "Be patient, then, brothers, until the Lord's coming. See how the farmer waits for the land to yield its valuable crop and how patient he is for the autumn and spring rains. You too, be patient and stand firm, because the Lord's coming is near" (James 5:7, 8). "As you know, we consider blessed those who have persevered" because "The Lord is full of compassion and mercy" (James 5:11).

Patience and hope are the fruit of distress. We glory in our tribulation, knowing that it produces patience which, teamed with experience, generates hope. "A few troubles and a little pain are good for us and help us to grow," said Wilfred A. Peters. "We should not complain that the rose bush has thorns, but should rejoice because it bears roses . . . ."

Never forget that God's ways are light years above our ways. We need to focus on the exhortation given by Paul, "we urge you, brothers, warn those who are idle, encourage the timid, help the weak, be patient with everyone" (1 Thessalonians 5:14).

Being patient with everyone implies true self-possession with inner quietness and calm. Don't confuse this quiet calm with resignation, which is simply passive submission. Being patient is an active, victorious exploit. To be patient, to bear suffering, to wait, to endure disappointment or trials with persistent moxie, to endure wrongs and evils done to you, to overlook petty annoyances, and to accomplish this without sinful reactions is a virtue to be sought after.

We have to practice cultivating the ability to accept positively, triumphantly what life hands us. And we have to accept ourselves with wholesomeness—realizing that we are "becomers," we're not yet what we will be. "To be what we are, and to become what we are capable of becoming is the only end of life," said Robert Louis Stevenson. So much of our impatience is due to our unwillingness to become who we are, without envying others or denigrating ourselves.

Patience begins with self-acceptance. We must take off the masks, and live in genuineness without regrets or resentments. You're not perfect. Is that news to anybody? Who among us is perfect? Once we admit our foibles, we can lighten up.

Once we accept ourselves without self-devaluation, without feeling it necessary to be demanding and hostile with others, then we can get on with the happier business of living with patience. We'll be free of the fear of rejection or humiliation. Arthur Guiterman wrote a short verse about this:

> Until the donkey tried to clear
>
> The fence, he thought himself a deer.

A donkey is not a deer, but it has no need to be envious; a deer did not carry Jesus into Jerusalem.

Besides accepting ourselves as we are, a great part of patience resides in letting others be what they are. In many years of marriage counseling, my Dad has noted again and again that "A lot of failing marriages could succeed if the partners would reach out in love to accept themselves and each other as they are—warts and all—and not try to cram each other into a pre-conceived mold."

As someone has wisely noted, "The altar is not a license to alter."

That's all very well and good. The theories sound promising. But how do you get from theory to reality?

You begin by accepting today resourcefully. Life is now—today—it's not some dreamed-of set of circumstances.

The abundant life in Christ does exist, but most of us are still at the stage where we'd just be thankful to survive. Fortunately, just surviving can carry us through to the abundant life. Here are some practical survival tips that work:

Act better than you feel. Don't be enslaved by your fickle emotions. Go ahead, act better than you feel—it's a very Christian thing to do.

I don't know what you're "feeling" right now. Actually, it's not important, because no matter what you're feeling it's not unique to you. We all share the same set of emotions. What you're wanting to know is whether life can change, whether you can change, and whether you can live in a way to make life give you good things.

The bottom of a pit is not a bad place to be. It gives you a clear view of up. Many a person has found God near enough when they became desperate enough.

But, here's a warning: If you look only at your *feelings*, you'll miss what God wants to give you. Having faith in Christ is not some feeling you get hold of. Faith is *choosing*—choosing to believe what God says, and then *doing* His will no matter how you feel. Feelings are not something we choose. They "just happen" to us. Neither you nor God needs to worry about your feelings. He looks only at your choices, your decisions.

So I urge you—choose to believe. Whether you feel like it or not, act as if you knew that the Good News is absolutely true for you. And choose to act better than you feel. Faith means walking through life in God's way, following His directions, believing that everything will turn out the way He says it will. Your feelings will follow along if you ignore them. "May the God of hope fill you with all joy and peace as you trust in him, so that you may overflow with hope by the power of the Holy Spirit" (Romans 15:13). He's saying that joy and peace come through believing—not before it.

After all, when do you feel better, before or after you take the needed medicine? Which faith saved Noah? The ark or his feelings?

Act better than you feel. Act more patient than you feel. "Fake it till you feel it." That's not trite advice. Sometimes we do have to fake it until the feeling is real; otherwise, we will be slaves to our wandering emotions.

Accept responsibility for your actions. It's always easier to blame someone else for our shortcomings than it is to accept the blame. "I wouldn't have to be so short-tempered if he/she didn't provoke me." The fact is, while I may be influenced by other people, I can't blame anybody else for my choices. I can't blame anybody else for my behavior. As Harry Truman said, "The buck stops here." The gospel tells us that each must give account of what he or she has done.

This also means that you're not overly responsible for what other people choose to do (assuming that you're seeking to behave as a Christian). How do good parents deal lovingly and patiently with rebellious children who throw away the values they were taught? What can you do, except patiently keep on doing what is right for you to do? Sometimes we have to let people suffer the consequences of their own choices. It calls for great patience to stand by and watch others make big mistakes—but sometimes that's all we can do.

Reach out to others. When I'm most impatient, I'm usually focused on myself. I lose sight of the fact that I'm really not the center of the universe. How do you break this self- centeredness? Dr. Karl Menninger was once asked, "What would you do if you thought you were losing your mind?" He answered, "The first thing I would do is go out and help somebody less fortunate than I am." When confronted with an occasion for impatience, turn the tables. Reach out and choose to do a kindness—right now—for the target of your impatience.

Believe even when you doubt. The tendency to seek "perfection or nothing" can lay a double whammy on our spiritual growth. It's one of Satan's best weapons against us. The truth is, if ours is a growing faith, then there are areas where it's not yet grown. The struggle to believe still goes on in some regions of the heart. Jesus told a man, "If you have faith I can heal your son." And the man responded for all of us—he exclaimed, "'I do believe; help me overcome my unbelief!'" (Mark 9:24). Faith and patience are a process. They grow from constant struggle.

You will become what you think about. That's what is meant by the old saying that every person's main duty is praise of God. By looking at Him, we are changed. Whatever gets your attention, gets you.

So here's the big question: Where are you looking? To what do you listen? To whom do you listen? What do you read? What are your daydreams made of? Do you give God the scraps and leftovers, or the first choice of all you are and have?

Scripture says that a fool's eyes are at the ends of the earth—anywhere except upon the God in whom he lives, moves, and has his very existence. God is the Beginning and the End of life. That's why Matthew (6:33) says, "Seek you first the kingdom of God, and his righteousness; and all these [other] things will be given to you." You know people who have a dream, who have a vision of what they are becoming. As the Nike shoe ads say, they "Just do it!" The mind reforms the person from within. "Do not conform any longer to the pattern of this world, but be transformed by the renewing of your mind. Then you will be able to test and approve what God's will is—his good, pleasing and perfect will" (Romans 12:2).

Paul finishes his letter to the Philippians with this admonition:

> Finally, brothers, whatever is true, whatever is noble, whatever is right, whatever is pure, whatever is lovely, whatever is admirable—if anything is excellent or praiseworthy—think about such things. Whatever you have learned or received or heard from me, or seen in me—put it into practice. And the God of peace will be with you (4:8-9).

When you think about such things, when you ponder such ideals, in time you become those things. Remember, whatever gets your attention, gets you. That's both a warning and a promise.

Be content. Near the end of his life, the apostle Paul writes to Timothy, his son in the faith. The advice is wise.

But godliness with contentment is great gain. For we brought nothing into the world, and we can take nothing out of it. But if we have food and clothing, we will be content with that. People who want to get rich fall into temptation and a trap and into many foolish and harmful desires that plunge men into ruin and destruction. For the love of money is a root of all kinds of evil. Some people, eager for money, have wandered from the faith and pierced themselves with many griefs

(1 Timothy 6:6-10).

Elsewhere he says,

I am not saying this because I am in need, for I have learned to be content whatever the circumstances. I know what it is to be in need, and I know what it is to have plenty. I have learned the secret of being content in any and every situation, whether well fed or hungry, whether living in plenty or in want. I can do everything through him who gives me strength (Philippians 4:11-13).

Contentment does not come from getting a promotion, buying a faster computer, owning a bigger house, or meeting a certain person. Contentment that is deep and satisfying is from Christ.

Make some plans for your life. In *Alice in Wonderland*, Alice asked the cat, "Would you tell me please, which way I ought to go from here?"

The cat replied, "That depends a good deal on where you want to go."

"Oh, I don't much care," said Alice. To which the cat responded,

"Then it doesn't matter much which way you go."

"But I want to go somewhere," protested Alice.

The cat answered with insight, "Oh, you are sure to do that."

It's amazing how many people have no goal, no purpose, no direction for life. The real need is for us to adopt God's plan for our life. You've heard people say, "I'm just turning everything over to the Lord." But this is one of the ways we shirk responsibility for our own actions. I don't think God is so concerned with whether I write an article for Magazine A or Magazine B (assuming both are honorable). But He is concerned with the focus and direction of my life and service to Him.

In retrospect, I can look back and see where things in my life "worked together for my good." But it sure is tough sometimes to see any pattern or plan from where things are happening in the here and now. I can see where I've been, and I can see that God's hand has been with me, but it's often tough to know what God's direction for me is at a given moment. Dr. Royce Money, president of Abilene Christian University, said, "I think God often gives us a set of choices and says, 'You choose, and I'll go with you.'"

Learn to handle your anger and impatience. This ability to resolve conflict is needed in all areas of life—it's needed by married couples, fellow workers, business associates, friends, enemies, governments, Christians, and whoever else you can name. James hit this nail on the head when he said, "We all stumble in many ways. If anyone is never at fault in what he says, he is a perfect man, able to keep his whole body in check" (James 3:2). We all know the amazing power in the words that roll off our tongue—power for good or ill. And after discussing that power, James goes on to say, "but no man can tame the tongue. It is a restless evil, full of deadly poison" (3:8).

It's impossible to talk and to really listen at the same time. Wouldn't a lot of our conflicts be more readily resolved if we started to really hear what the other person was saying? Not just his or her words, but what they were trying to communicate to us. It's difficult to argue with someone who is listening well enough to understand you.

Be the peacemaker. This one will test your determination. We're talking about going out on a limb, going first, doing the thing that needs doing. Somebody has to say, "I'm sorry." Christians are a people who live agape love, which means that we are to seek the good of the other person or the relationship. And that demands that you go first and say "I'm sorry."

"Blessed are the peacemakers, for they will be called sons of God" (Matthew 5:9). It's a way that works. It's a higher, heaven- inspired way. It's the way to the abundant life. But it will call for your greatest determination to take this way of going first. You're going to find yourself in those eyeball-to-eyeball confrontations sometimes. It's inevitable. The question is, who's going first. Remember, the truest test of moral courage is the ability to ignore the insult. Be big. Go first. No one is too big to go first, but some are too small.

You will have your reward. When we want to get to the heart of a matter, a current expression says "Cut to the chase." Jesus was good at "cutting to the chase." He takes us right to the point when He says, "I will show you what he is like who comes to me and hears my words and puts them into practice" (Luke 6:47). "The proof of the pudding is in the eating," and the reward for right behavior is in the doing.

Thinking right is important, attitudes do make a difference, and motives do affect us. But these guides for improving our "PQ" (Patience Quotient) have come full circle. So, the next time your goat gets got and you *feel* impatient, that's the time to act better than you feel about the situation—and you will receive the reward that comes from doing right.

CHAPTER 10

When Patience Runs Out

Aren't you thankful that God isn't short tempered? If He were an impatient God, I would have been pulverized long ago. He has been patient with me far beyond the limits to which I'm able to go with my "fellow servants." But we're still working on me. As writers like to say, I'm still "a work in progress."

Patience, endurance, constancy, steadfastness, perseverance, forbearance, long suffering, slowness in avenging wrongs—it is the endurance of wrong without anger or retaliation. The person who is patient will bear with the weaknesses of others.

Real patience is not merely a shallow good nature. No way! It is a mighty and dynamic fruit of the Spirit that makes for love and peace, enabling us to bear injury without taking vengeance.

Makrothumia, that Greek word for patience, is used in the Septuagint version of the Old Testament to translate a Hebrew phrase meaning "slow to anger": "The Lord is slow to anger, abounding in love and forgiving sin and rebellion" (Numbers 14:18a).

In the New Testament there is the familiar passage: "The Lord is not slow in keeping his promise, as some understand slowness. He is patient with you, not wanting anyone to perish, but everyone to come to repentance" (2 Peter 3:9). He doesn't ignore the evil we do. Instead, like a wise parent, He knows when to look the other way—when to "not notice" what we just did. He reacts differently to provocation than we do. God is waiting with restraint, giving us time to change our ways.

And if He has again and again shown us His patience, how can we not extend patience to others? As we noted earlier, Divine and human patience go hand in hand—*quid pro quo*. Against the background of Divine "slowness to anger," it is surely inappropriate for us to be short tempered and impatient with anybody. Unless we are patient and merciful, God will eventually withhold His patience from us, because "what goes around comes around." That's not Scripture, but it's truth.

Lest we miss the point in all the examples of Godly patience, He goes on to make sure we get the message—He directs us to exercise patience: "Be joyful in hope, patient in affliction, faithful in prayer," Paul writes to the Christians in Rome (Romans 12:12).

And the Lord again emphasizes the necessity of patience by informing us that if we are abiding in Him, then patience is an inevitable result, because " . . . the fruit of the Spirit is love, joy, peace, patience, kindness, goodness, faithfulness" (Galatians 5:22).

And James urges his readers, "Be patient, then, brothers, until the Lord's coming" (James 5:7).

Peter reinforces the prerequisite of patience:

Through these he has given us his very great and precious

promises, so that through them you may participate in the divine nature and escape the corruption in the world caused by evil desires. For this very reason, make every effort to add to your faith goodness; and to goodness, knowledge; and to knowledge, self-control; and to self-control, perseverance; and to perseverance, godliness; and to godliness, brotherly kindness; and to brotherly kindness, love (2 Peter 1:4-7).

Patience is essential to our salvation. "By standing firm you will gain life" (Luke 21:19). Or, as the King James Version words it, "In your patience ye shall win your souls." Life is a battleground in the war between good and evil. So, "Let us not become weary in doing good, for at the proper time we will reap a harvest if we do not give up" (Galatians 6:9). We must have endurance for the duration. Remember, it is never right to do wrong, and it's never wrong to do right.

And having said all of that, suddenly we flip the coin over and discover that it also has a reverse: Patience has a rightful limit.

While our impatience is often hurtful, and while patience is required of us, nevertheless patience does have a limit. Longsuffering does not imply, nor does it include interminable distress.

God demonstrates this in dealing with His people through the ages. Listen to the prophet Nehemiah:

> They refused to listen and failed to remember the miracles you performed among them. They became stiff-necked and in their rebellion appointed a leader in order to return to their slavery. But you are a forgiving God, gracious and compassionate, slow to anger and abounding in love. Therefore you did not desert them . . . (Nehemiah 9:17).

But God's patience was finally exhausted. "For many years you were patient with them," said the prophet. "By your

Spirit you admonished them through your prophets. Yet they paid no attention, so you handed them over to the neighboring peoples" (Nehemiah 9:30).

God does not leave the *unrepentant* unpunished. "The LORD is slow to anger, abounding in love and forgiving sin and rebellion. Yet he does not leave the guilty unpunished; he punishes the children for the sin of the fathers to the third and fourth generation" (Numbers 14:18). That old covenant was a tight shoe to wear.

Being long-fused is not the same as having no fuse. At a certain point, God takes no more from His creatures. He leaves us to our own devices and permits us to create our own ruin. He judges us for our sin and unwillingness to turn from it. Read what Paul wrote to the church in Rome:

> For although they knew God, they neither glorified him as God nor gave thanks to him, but their thinking became futile and their foolish hearts were darkened. Although they claimed to be wise, they became fools and exchanged the glory of the immortal God for images made to look like mortal man and birds and animals and reptiles. Therefore God gave them over in the sinful desires of their hearts to sexual impurity for the degrading of their bodies with one another . . . Because of this, God gave them over to shameful lusts (Romans 1:21-24, 26).

It isn't a license for impatience, but there comes a time when we must be like God in this respect. We must have enough character and enough understanding of good and evil so that after we have been patient, tolerant, kind, and loving, we finally draw the line. Out of respect for God and all that is holy you must say, "This is the limit." Out of respect for your God-given human dignity you should declare, "I must not take any more."

Where the line is for me is not easy for you to judge. And

I can't readily referee your decision on this. No hard-and-fast rules have been laid down for this matter.

Do you remember the story of the divorce court judge? One day his docket included the case of the 89-year-old woman suing her 92-year-old husband for divorce after seventy years of marriage. The judge couldn't believe it. "Do you mean that after all these years you can't patch up this marriage?" he asked incredulously. To which the old woman replied, "Your honor, enough's enough."

On a more realistic level, at some point, a wife who has been patient and loving with a rascal of a husband is justified in giving up on him. At some point—in order to protect herself physically and spiritually, in order to save her children from abuse or from hell, she may have to leave the marriage. At some point, enough's enough.

Sometimes a child who has been patient with parents has to leave home in the name of self-preservation. And sometimes parents who have been patient with their child have to say through their tears, "We will not, and cannot bear more of this. You cannot stay in our house." The whole concept of "Tough Love" has been formulated to deal with these rough choices. At some point, enough's enough.

Sometimes the church, which is to be the bedrock of patience, gentleness, and love, has to say, "No more!" In Matthew 18 the Lord gives us a procedure to use when one in the body sins: Go to the brother or sister, tell him his or her sin, and ask him to repent. If he doesn't, then be patient. Take two others with you and let them plead with the person. When that doesn't work, keep being patient. Ask the whole church to help. If the person won't hear the church and persists in sin, withdraw your fellowship from him or her. We cannot be patient beyond the point at which God will be patient. At some point, enough's enough.

Paul required the church at Corinth to excommunicate a brother who was guilty of incest—and impenitent. And the church itself boasted of its tolerance.

> It is actually reported that there is sexual immorality among you, and of a kind that does not occur even among pagans: A man has his father's wife. And you are proud! Shouldn't you rather have been filled with grief and have put out of your fellowship the man who did this? Even though I am not physically present, I am with you in spirit. And I have already passed judgment on the one who did this, just as if I were present. When you are assembled in the name of our Lord Jesus and I am with you in spirit, and the power of our Lord Jesus is present, hand this man over to Satan, so that the sinful nature may be destroyed and his spirit saved on the day of the Lord (1 Corinthians 5:1-5).

Sometimes we have to do the same thing. It isn't because someone has made us angry, or hurt us personally, and we want to get back at them. This is where we must show patience. But when it becomes obvious that a person isn't repenting and that the sinful behavior isn't due to ignorance or immaturity, then the line must be drawn. When lying, drunkenness, marital unfaithfulness, false teaching, is deliberate and persistent, a faithful body of believers must say, "No more!" At some point, enough's enough.

> I have written you in my letter not to associate with sexually immoral people—not at all meaning the people of this world who are immoral, or the greedy and swindlers, or idolaters. In that case you would have to leave this world. But now I am writing you that you must not associate with anyone who calls himself a brother but is sexually immoral or greedy, an idolater or a slanderer, a drunkard or a swindler. With such a man do not even eat. What business is it of mine to judge those outside the church? Are you not to judge those inside? God will judge those outside. "Expel the wicked man from among you" (1 Corinthians 5:9-13).

At some point, enough's enough.

This aspect of patience is not one we're comfortable with, but it is part of the picture. When should patience run out? Where is the limit of patience? When do you draw the line?

The impatience of Paul could have cost the church the services of Mark. You remember in the book of Acts that Paul was unhappy with the young man's turning back home during the first missionary journey. But Barnabas had the wisdom to counsel and guide John Mark through this immature period of his growth. Eventually, even Paul said that Mark "is profitable to me."

There is a line to be drawn sometimes. It can be drawn too soon. It can be drawn for the wrong reasons. But still, with prayer and patience, at some point, enough's enough.

CHAPTER 11
I Need Help In the Kitchen

Patience is the ability to idle your motor when you feel like stripping your gears.

Call it the "Lone Ranger Syndrome," but it's really aggravating to feel like you're the only person tending to the business at hand.

You remember the account in Luke 10:38-42, where Jesus and His disciples were walking through the village where Mary, Martha, and Lazarus opened their home to him. Mary was captivated by the teaching and conversation of Jesus, and she sat at the Lord's feet listening to what He said. But Martha was a practical-minded lady. With all these guests in her house, there was work to be done. Luke says that Martha was "distracted by all the preparations that had to be made." She came to Jesus and asked, "Lord, don't you care that my sister has left me to do the work by myself? Tell her to help me!"

"Martha, Martha," answered the Lord, "you are worried and upset about many things, but only one thing is needed. Mary has chosen what is better, and it will not be taken away from her."

Martha was impatient with Mary—and with Jesus. And I can understand her impatience. When you're knocking yourself out working, or doing "the necessary thing," and everybody else is goofing off, your righteous indignation can sure flare up. We all tend to act like Martha now and then. There was nothing wrong with what she was doing—preparing food. And there wasn't anything out of line in her wanting Mary to help her do the necessary things. But this is one of those times when there was a better option. Think about it: is it better to prepare an attractive, tasty meal, or to take advantage of a once-in-a-lifetime opportunity to learn at the feet of the Master Teacher?

Where does patience come from? Where does it lead us?

Mary and Martha show us that impatience can lead us away from the Lord, while waiting for Him with patience can bring us nearer to His feet.

God expects patience from His people. "Be still before the Lord and wait patiently for him" (Psalm 37:7). "Be joyful in hope, patient in affliction, faithful in prayer," Paul writes to the Christians in Rome (Romans 12:12). Patience is a facet of God's dealing with humanity, His creatures: " . . . do you show contempt for the riches of his kindness, tolerance and patience, not realizing that God's kindness leads you toward repentance?" (Romans 2:4).

God's own Holy Spirit engenders patience in those who are under His influence and control: " . . . The fruit of the Spirit is love, joy, peace, patience, kindness, goodness, faithfulness" (Galatians 5:22).

Patience comes from God, but a lot depends on our perception of Him, ourselves, and others.

I once read a maxim which said, "If you have an impatient neighbor, chances are that he does too."

Have you ever thought much about the fact that life reflects back to you a true picture of yourself? That's how it works. "To the pure, all things are pure, but to those who are corrupted and do not believe, nothing is pure. In fact, both their minds and consciences are corrupted" (Titus 1:15). Life is a mirror of our own thinking. When we understand this principle, we can call on God to help us renew our minds in Him, making the needed changes within ourselves—knowing that our view of life will show us an evolving reflection of the precise degree of our own renewal.

It's a funny thing, but things turn out best for those who make the best of the way things turn out.

If you're happy with your world, it's a sign that you're a happy person. If people are patient with you, it's an evidence that you show patience to others. There will be bad times, of course, because that's part of living. But impatience doesn't attack as often, or as bad for the person with a patient frame of mind toward himself and life. People who find themselves treated impatiently most of the time should understand this is a sign that they themselves are impatient. We need to reshape our thinking—find something to do to exercise patience. Do something good for an ungrateful, unappreciative person. And as your own patience is exercised, new patience will enter your world.

The trick is in seeing that we must first become that which we seek to possess. Before molten steel can be formed into a useful working tool, a mold or stamp must first be shaped. Before a house can be constructed, a foundation mirroring the outlines must be formed. And before a person can find life to be as he or she desires, he must first become that kind of person. We are charged with responsibility for the cause, and the effect follows naturally—and it never fails to happen.

That's what Paul wrote to the Corinthians when he said, " . . . we, who with unveiled faces all reflect the Lord's glory, are being transformed into his likeness with ever-increasing glory, which comes from the Lord, who is the Spirit" (2 Corinthians 3:18). When our minds dwell long enough on the features of a spiritual image, we become that very image.

And when we view life and its struggles from the perspective of eternity, we can clearly see that " . . . our light and momentary troubles are achieving for us an eternal glory that far outweighs them all" (2 Corinthians 4:17). Patience is a more obtainable commodity when seen from eternity's shore.

Everything happens because of the law of cause and effect. A good cause produces a good effect. A bad cause generates a bad effect. That's why it's true that life heaps impatience on the heads of impatient people. When my sister was a little girl, she used to say "Turnabout is turnabout." And I think she was right. The effect can only reflect the cause.

But isn't it astounding how few of us really comprehend the implications of this simple rule! It's literally a law of nature. We go through life, being treated harshly, with impatience, by everybody we run into—without understanding that life can only react to us (we are the "cause," and our life experience is the "effect"). My world is a mirror image of my true self. Your world is a reflection of your true self. If we don't like the reflection (life), understand that it can't change until we do.

And somebody will say, "That's just my personality, I can't do anything about it." Or, "My situation is different, I'm justified in being short tempered." Balderdash!—as my niece responded one time at age two. That's an irresponsible attitude, guaranteed to make you miserable. With God and the Spirit to sustain us, and with Christ as a pattern, we can change, we can be transformed by the renewing of our minds. The Lord doesn't torment us with commands that we aren't able to keep, and He instructs us through Paul, "Therefore, as God's chosen people, holy and dearly loved, clothe yourselves with compassion, kindness, humility, gentleness and patience" (Colossians 3:12).

So we can become people with patience—if we seek to do that. The experts say that the best way to start is to act like the person you'd like to become. Begin playing the part, and actually act out the role of the person you want to be. Actions trigger feelings, just like feelings trigger actions. When you act a certain way long enough, you will literally build the propensity for being that type of person. Once this is accomplished, the life which that type of person would have will come to you.

The wise man in Proverbs stressed this axiom. "A patient man has great understanding," he said, "but a quick-tempered man displays folly" (Proverbs 14:29). "A hot-tempered man stirs up dissension, but a patient man calms a quarrel" (15:18).

Where you find an impatient person, you find dissension abounding; but, where you find a patient person, you find calm.

This is how a wise person transforms his world—just as a potter shapes the mound of clay—and builds it into the life which is most satisfying. It's not an effortless job. It requires time—and perseverance. But it's a task worth the effort. If you like the way your world treats you, that's good. You're to be congratulated, because you've discovered the secret of a happy life. But if you don't like the way your world treats you, begin transforming yourself into the kind of person you would really want to be, and your world will change with you.

Harold Sherman, quite awhile ago, wrote a book entitled *How To Turn Failure Into Success*. In it he gives a "Code of Persistence." If you find yourself giving up too easily—on yourself, on others, or on events—write this down and read it daily.

1. I will never give up so long as I know I am right.
2. I will believe that all things will work out for me if I hang on until the end.
3. I will be courageous and undismayed in the face of odds.
4. I will not permit anyone to intimidate me or deter me from my goals.
5. I will fight to overcome all physical handicaps and setbacks.
6. I will try again and again and yet again to accomplish what I desire.
7. I will take new faith and resolution from the knowledge that all successful men and women had to fight defeat and adversity.
8. I will never surrender to discouragement or despair no matter what seeming obstacles may confront me.

Life is like a river. Everything that flows into my life or your life becomes part of us. But we possess a marvelous power of selection, and we can determine which streams we will accept and which we will reject. And those choices carry far reaching implications.

There's an interesting exchange in Lewis Carroll's *Alice in Wonderland*—

ALICE: Where I come from, people study what they are NOT good at in order to be able to do what they ARE good at.

MAD HATTER: We only go around in circles here in Wonderland, but we always end up where we started. Would you mind explaining yourself?

ALICE: Well, grown-ups tell us to find out what

we did wrong and never do it again.

MAD HATTER: That's odd! It seems to me that in order to find out about something you have to study it. And when you study it, you should become better at it. Why should you want to become better at something and then never do it again? But please continue.

ALICE: Nobody ever tells us to study the right things we do. We're only supposed to learn from the wrong things. But we are permitted to study the right things OTHER people do. And sometimes we're even told to copy them.

MAD HATTER: That's cheating!

ALICE: You're quite right, Mr. Hatter. I do live in a topsy-turvy world. It seems like I have to do something wrong first, in order to learn from that what not to do. And then, by not doing what I'm not supposed to do, perhaps I'll be right. But I'd rather be right the first time, wouldn't you?

It sounds as though Alice was contemplating which streams to allow to feed the river of her life. The tributaries that pour their contents into a river determine the quality and flow of that river. So do the streams of influence which flow into your life and mine. They determine our thoughts and deeds. This is a natural law as old as time and as binding as the law of gravity, but we still tend to believe that we can break it and not suffer the consequences.

There is one big difference to the comparison of life being

like a river: a river has no control over the streams that flow into it. Gravity irresistibly draws streams downward toward the river. Even if the river is crystal clear at its source, its streams may fill it with muddy, chemically polluted, sewage tainted waste water. That which was pure and clear becomes dirty and impure—and has no say in the matter. Anything flowing into the watershed of that river ends up in the river without any pause for rejection.

It's different with us. Like the river, all that flows into life becomes part of us, but we have a God-given choice of selection. This is where Mary and Martha differed that day Jesus came to visit. We can determine which of those streams we will accept or reject. We can't accept every stream flowing our way or else the river of life would be forever out of its banks. And we can't refuse all of the streams which life sends us or else we'd soon be a dried-up riverbed. Instead, we must control the stream and channel its flow with a constant accepting and rejecting of various tributaries.

Several years ago, country singer Willie Nelson recorded a song called "Take Me As I Am, Or Let Me Go." Many people try to exonerate their impatience and justify their angry conduct by thinking "That's just me, and you take me or leave me—as is." They assume that these streams of impatience must flow into their lives, and that by expressing crabbiness they are at least honest—not hypocrites. They turn a vice into a "virtue."

We hear the saying, "Take me as I am, warts and all."

That's actually an attitude to be taken by the other party in that deal. If I choose to accept you—warts and all—it may be a commendable attitude on my part. But for you to inflict hurtful, unpleasant behavior upon me and then shirk responsibility for your own shortcomings by saying "Take me as I am, warts and all" is another matter.

This isn't reality and truth in Christ. You are not required to "muddy up" your life with streams of impatience. That's a choice you make, and you can make a right one or a wrong one.

Thank God we aren't left to our own strengths and devices when it comes to all of this. Paul was the one who showed us that "I can do everything through him who gives me strength" (Philippians 4:13).

This apostle wrote to the Christians at Colosse (Colossians 1:1-14), saying,

> . . . We always thank God . . . when we pray for you, because we have heard of your faith in Christ Jesus and of the love you have for all the saints—the faith and love that spring from the hope that is stored up for you in heaven and that you have already heard about in the word of truth, the gospel that has come to you. All over the world this gospel is bearing fruit and growing, just as it has been doing among you since the day you heard it and understood God's grace in all its truth . . . For this reason . . . , we have not stopped praying for you and asking God to fill you with the knowledge of his will through all spiritual wisdom and understanding. And we pray this in order that you may live a life worthy of the Lord and may please him in every way: bearing fruit in every good work, growing in the knowledge of God, being strengthened with all power according to his glorious might so that you may have great endurance and patience, and joyfully giving thanks to the Father, who has qualified you to share in the inheritance of the saints in the kingdom of light. For he has rescued us from the dominion of darkness and brought us into the kingdom of the Son he loves, in whom we have redemption, the forgiveness of sins.

Now there's a stream we need in the river of life. It tells us a lot we need to know. It says that faith and love spring from hope. When determination and willpower begin to drag, our hope for heaven can support faith and renew our love. The gospel, the word of truth, calls us to live a life worthy of the

Lord. Then Paul shows us what that worthy life includes: it has the fruit of good actions, a growing knowledge of God, and a strengthening with His power. God's power is clearly evident in the lives of His people. While some want to believe that this power is evidenced by miraculous "gifts of the Spirit"— tongue-speaking, healing, divine knowledge—it seems to me that Paul goes on to show us how God's power is seen in His people. Paul says that God's power gives us "endurance and patience."

Endurance and patience for what?—"to share in the inheritance of the saints in the kingdom of light." What is that inheritance? "We have redemption, the forgiveness of sins."

That's not as melodramatic, mysterious, or entertaining as some expectations of God's power, but it performs as advertised. All the time. Every time. The great purpose of living should be eternal salvation, and God will empower us with everything we need—including the patience and endurance— for achieving that goal.

CHAPTER 12
"Wait For It"

I'm a devotee of the old *M*A*S*H* reruns on television. If you've watched the show, you're familiar with the character Radar O'Reilly.

He's called Radar because he senses events before others have become aware of them. As a frontline hospital unit in the Korean conflict, the doctors of *M*A*S*H* received many of their wounded patients via helicopter. In the middle of all sorts of activities and noises, Radar would say, "Oh, oh. We've got wounded."

Everybody would pause, listening for distant helicopters, and somebody would say, "I don't hear anything."

To which Radar would respond, "Wait for it." And he was always right.

You say that you want patience? You can have it. Patience is only a matter of time. Wait for it.

"The trouble with you, Son," said the father to his teenager, "is that you're always hoping for things you don't have."

"That's true, Dad—but what else would I hope for?"

"But if we hope for what we do not yet have, we wait for it patiently" (Romans 8:25).

This must be history's most impatient generation. Nations are concerned about economic woes, impatiently seeking quick fixes. "Little" wars rage, demonstrating humanity's terrible ill-temper when it comes to solving regional and national disputes. There is concern over the environment and energy resources. There's a sense of panic in practically every news story from Washington to Timbuktu. How can we possibly live in patient trust like "a tree planted by the waters"?

"That's okay for people with ordinary problems, but I'm overloaded with major troubles I can't do anything about and I need answers right now."

Isn't that our state of mind?

But the Psalmist says, "Cast your cares on the LORD and he will sustain you; he will never let the righteous fall" (Psalm 55:22).

God isn't joking when he says to trust Him. He's not like Lucy in the *Peanuts* comic strip, perennially coaxing Charlie Brown into kicking the football one more time—then at the last second yanking it away and taunting "Gotcha!" The apostle Paul knew the meaning of distress and hardship, but he said "If God is for us, who is against us?" Paul was certain that he had committed the ebb and flow of his life to the all-powerful and loving God.

The tragedy is that we live as if we had to solve our problems with our own feeble strength. Truly blessed is the person who can let go of his own timetable for solving things, and "wait for it" while watching God work. He will supply the patience and endurance if we will place our hope in His hands.

Lord, help us hear your steadfast love today, because we trust only you. Show us the way to go, because we worship only you.

Snoopy, the little terrier dog I used to have, was dedicated to only two pursuits: eating heartily, and running to every activity as if a demon were at her tail. She loved fetching her rubber ball with the bell rattling inside. She evaluated people by their willingness to play ball until she tired of the game. It didn't matter whether folks had a grandma arm or a Nolan Ryan pitch, as long as they would play.

Watching Snoopy, I witnessed a joy for living that exploded into action the minute she saw an opportunity to play ball with a friend. There was never any impatience or sulking when nobody was around to throw the ball, but there was a special vitality that came forth when the occasion presented itself.

The last chapter of the book *Psycho-Cybernetics*, by the late Maxwell Maltz, has done wonders for a lot of people. It talks about the kind of energy for life which Snoopy authenticated. To paraphrase one of the book's ideas, you can say that if life can be adapted in many different ways as a means toward an end, isn't it sensible to believe that if we put ourselves in the sorts of situations where more life is needed, we will get more life? Couldn't the same be said for patience? If we think of ourselves as goal-seekers, we can think of "adaptation energy" as that which drives us toward a goal.

Maltz borrowed the term "adaptation energy" from Dr. Hans Selye, the well-known expert on stress. "Life force" was the term Maltz used. Either way, even the unredeemed "natural man" seems to have extra energy for achieving when there's motivation to release it. And when the believer is empowered by the Lord with His patience and endurance, the result seems greater than the mere sum of the parts.

There is strength for endurance available to believers. The

source is the Holy Spirit, channeled to us through the Word of the Spirit. When we cooperate with God, we receive an inner energy and ability to do His will for our life. "I know what it is to be in need," said Paul, "and I know what it is to have plenty. I have learned the secret of being content in any and every situation, whether well fed or hungry, whether living in plenty or in want. I can do everything through him who gives me strength" (Philippians 4:12, 13).

Everything? Could Paul flap his arms and fly wherever he wanted to go? Of course not. His missionary journeys were made via the same transportation modes used by everybody else. When he said "I can do everything," Paul was talking about everything he needed to do in order to live out God's will for him. That same empowerment can be ours as well.

God is limited in what He can do for some people because of their impatience, which causes them to run ahead of His leading. If you intend to hold onto anger and impatience, God cannot help you overcome them.

This prose verse powerfully expresses the idea of turning yourself over to the Lord's control:

The Road of Life

At first, I saw God as my observer, my judge,
keeping track or the things I did wrong,
so as to know whether I merited heaven
or hell when I die.
He was out there sort of like a president.
I recognized His picture when I saw it,
but I really didn't know Him.

But later on
when I met Christ, it seemed as though
life were rather like a bike ride,
and I noticed that Christ

was in the back helping me pedal.

I don't know just when it was
that he suggested we change places,
but life has not been the same since.
When I had control,
I knew the way.
It was rather boring,
but predictable . . .
It was the shortest distance between two points.

But when He took the lead,
He knew delightful long cuts,
up mountains,
and through rocky places
at breakneck speeds.
Even though it looked like madness,
He said, "Pedal!"

I worried and was anxious
and asked,
"Where are you taking me?"
He laughed and didn't answer,
and I started to learn to trust.

I forgot my boring life
and entered into the adventure.
And when I'd say, "I'm scared,"
He'd lean back and touch my hand.

He took me to people with gifts that
I needed, gifts of healing,
acceptance
and joy.
They gave me gifts to take on my journey,
my Lord's and mine.

And we were off again.

He said, "Give the gifts away;
they're extra baggage, too much weight."
So I did,
to people we met,
and I found that in giving I received,
and still our burden was light.

I did not trust Him,
at first,
in control of my life.
I thought He'd wreck it;
but He knows bike secrets,
knows how to make it bend to take sharp corners,
knows how to jump to clear high rocks,
knows how to fly to shorten scary passages.

And I am learning to shut up
and pedal
in the strangest places,
and I'm beginning to enjoy the view
and the cool breeze on my face
with my delightful constant companion, Jesus Christ.
And when I'm sure I just can't do
anymore, He just smiles and says . . . "Pedal."

—author unknown

Turning loose is good for you. Right thinking—hope, faith, patience—improves your being in four ways: spiritually, mentally, emotionally, and even physically. The delightful blend of our positive attitudes and the work of the Holy Spirit is a winning duo. Something good is bound to happen when we cooperate with God this way.

In his book *How to Live 365 Days a Year*, Dr. John A. Schindler identifies six basic human needs. Each of us needs love, security, creative expression, recognition, new experiences, and self-esteem.

The prime need for love seems to be fulfilled when you focus on showing love to others rather than waiting for someone to show love to you.

Most people have to work to obtain material security because various realities of life must be faced—no work, no pay.

Creative expression is not always recognized as a basic need; however, creativity is deeply satisfying to our inner self and effort spent on it is very rewarding.

Recognition generally comes our way when we earn it, and you won't need to blow your own horn to get it.

New experiences are vital to our well-being, and yet we dread them in a lot of cases. Whether you view them as crises or opportunities, you're still going to face changes and new situations throughout life. Being born is a life-changing event, and that's only the beginning. As a child, you must start school, change schools, move to a new home, accept the arrival of new siblings, lose friends who move away, lose a pet, and lose loved ones (to death, divorce, desertion). Teenagers encounter the trauma of moving, breaking up, parents' divorce, personal crises (pregnancy, illness, injury), failure in school, losing jobs, and the loss of friends or family to death. Adults face "new experiences" in marriage, having children, divorce, starting careers, losing jobs, changing jobs, illness, disability, aging, retirement, poverty, loss of independence, and the death of friends and loved ones.

We can deal with life changes in several ways: denial, depression and withdrawal, escape through drugs and alcohol, escape through pleasure and self-indulgence, take a Pollyanna attitude, lash out in rage, or resort to suicide. Notice that the thing which is missing in each of those reactions is patient endurance. None of those self-centered responses includes waiting on the Lord. But if we approach life's new passages with faith in the Lord and a trust in our ultimate victory, we'll be ready for new experiences.

Our basic need for self-esteem is one of those things that's up to us. A good self-image does wonders for your Patience Quotient. You can help your self-esteem by looking at each new day as a fresh opportunity. Remember, yesterday is a canceled check; tomorrow is a promissory note; today is the only cash you have. So no matter what has happened in the past, and no matter what you wish would happen in the future, this present moment is the only opportunity you'll ever have for doing God's will. Today is the only day you'll have for demonstrating patient endurance. "Today is the day of salvation."

It's a matter of hope, of knowledge, of desire. Patience comes from a willingness to wait for the Lord's schedule to become clear. But you have to "Wait for it."

"You can't plant corn in the morning and have roasting ears for dinner," as the old proverb says. Let's patiently await the Lord's coming and our heavenly inheritance. "We do not want you to become lazy, but to imitate those who through faith and patience inherit what has been promised" (Hebrews 6:12). "So do not throw away your confidence; it will be richly rewarded. You need to persevere so that when you have done the will of God, you will receive what he has promised" (Hebrews 10:35, 36). "Praise be to the God and Father of our Lord Jesus Christ! In his great mercy he has given us new birth into a living hope through the resurrection of Jesus Christ from the dead, and into an inheritance that can never perish, spoil or fade—kept in heaven for you" (1 Peter 1:3, 4). "But if we hope for what we do not yet have, we wait for it patiently" (Romans 8:25).

Heaven is our hope. It's worth waiting for. The best fruit ripens the slowest.

Strive for patience in prayer. The Lord sometimes responds to our prayer requests by saying, "Wait for it." He often chooses to take more time than we like in working out the wonders of His will. And sometimes He overrides our wants.

David asked God to let him build a temple for Him, but the Lord said no, "'Solomon your son is the one who will build my house and my courts, for I have chosen him to be my son, and I will be his father'" (1 Chronicles 28:6).

Even the coming of Christ into our world was done on God's infinite schedule: "But when the time had fully come, God sent his Son, born of a woman, born under law" (Galatians 4:4).

Answers to our prayers may need to be delayed if we're not quite ready to receive them, or we may need more strengthening of our perseverance—to cleanse our alloys and imperfections. And God's own immutable laws may need more time to operate. God's delays are not necessarily God's denials, so hold on. Wait for it. " . . . I waited patiently for the LORD; he turned to me and heard my cry" (Psalms 40:1).

Patience will keep us from doing regrettable things. A story is told about Dr. Blaikie, the Scottish professor, who once spoke very sharply and severely to one of his reciting students for not holding the book in his right hand. Later, Blaikie discovered that the young man had no right hand. A little more patience could have prevented this awkward and painful misunderstanding.

We sometimes get bogged down in problems, but amazingly they're seldom as bad as they seem. Test pilots have a quick method for evaluating sudden emergencies. Alan Bean, retired Apollo Astronaut, says when something goes wrong, test pilots ask, "Is this thing still flying?" If the answer is yes, then there's no immediate danger, no need to overreact. When Apollo 12 blasted off, the spacecraft was hit by lightning. The entire flight console began glowing with orange and red warning lights. "There was a temptation to 'Do Something,'" said Bean. But the pilots asked themselves, "Is this thing still flying in the right direction?" The answer was yes—it was headed for the moon. They let the lights glow as they addressed the individual problems, and watched orange and red lights blink out, one by one. That's something to think about in any pressure situation. If your thing is still flying, think first, and then act.

"Patience strengthens the spirit," someone has said, "sweetens the temper, stifles anger, extinguishes envy, subdues pride, bridles the tongue, restrains the hand, and tramples upon temptation." Wait for it.

In front of me, in my bookcase, are six sculpted eagles. Three are porcelain, one is silver, one is wood, and one is bronze. I enjoy looking at them. There's something lofty and majestic about eagles. They inspire me to the heights. As God's creation, they do something which I, as a human, have yet to accomplish: in their soaring, high, and grand endeavors they always live in perfect harmony with the Creator's design for them. They always are about the business of doing what God designed them to do. That's magnificent. But it's also the only response they can make to life. Unlike the human part of the creation, eagles are not free-will beings. Only you and I are endowed with the power to choose between good and evil—to choose between patience and impatience.

There's a song called "Teach Me, Lord, To Wait." (© 1953 R 1981 by Hamlen Music Co). It's based on Isaiah 40:31, and it's a favorite of mine. The words say,

> Teach me, Lord, to wait,
> Down on my knees,
> 'Till in your own good time
> You answer my pleas.

Teach me not to rely
On what others do,
But to wait in prayer
For an answer from You.

Chorus
"They that wait upon the Lord
Shall renew their strength;
They shall mount up with wings as eagles;
They shall run, and not be weary;
They shall walk, and not faint."
Teach me, Lord, Teach me, Lord, to wait.

Teach me, Lord, to wait
While hearts are aflame.
Let me humble my pride,
And call on Your name.

Keep my faith renewed,
My eyes on Thee.
Let me be on this earth,
What You want me to be.

Repeat Chorus
"They that wait upon the Lord
Shall renew their strength;
They shall mount up with wings as eagles;
They shall run, and not be weary;
They shall walk, and not faint."
Teach me, Lord, Teach me, Lord, to wait.

Amen.